ISSUES IN GENDER,

LANGUAGE LEARNING,

AND

CLASSROOM PEDAGOGY

EDITED BY

Effie Papatzikou Cochran, Ed.D.
John Jay College of Criminal Justice
CUNY, New York

Mary Yepez, Ph.D.
Bergen Community College
New Jersey

PUBLISHED IN COLLABORATION
NJTESOL - NJBE
&
Bastos Educational Publications

This is the second of a series of monographs intended to present recent scholarship in the field of ESL/EFL, Bilingual Education, and Multiculturalism. As such, this publication is addressed to interested professionals in the field of education who are concerned with issues in English language teaching, language teacher education, gender language practices, and related areas.

Published in collaboration:

© **NJTESOL – NJBE**
New Jersey Teachers of English to Speakers of Other Languages – Bilingual Educators
&
Bastos Educational Publications
P. O. Box 770-433
Woodside, NY 11377
1-800-662-0301
Fax: (718) 997-6445

www. **bastosbooks**.com
e-mail: **bastos@bastosbooks**.com

The publishers would like to thank all those who generously provided guidance and encouragement to help shape and improve the quality of this monograph and sincerely appreciate their contributions.

First published 2001

Printed in the United States of America

ISBN 1-883514-05-3

➤ *NJTESOL-NJBE Monograph Editorial Director*
Mihri Napoliello, Ed.D.

➤ *Publisher*
Genaro Bastos, M.A., M.Ed.

➤ *Managing Editor*
Mara Cordal-Bastos, M.A.

➤ *Graphic Design*
Prints 'N' Graphics, Inc., Rego Park, NY

Dedication

This volume is dedicated to the memory of Myra Sadker in gratitude for her lifelong work on gender equity in education. She is sorely missed by all who have been exposed to her and her husband's teaching, workshops, and publications.

TABLE OF CONTENTS

Foreword i

Overview iii

Acknowledgements vi

A Synthesis of Existing Research on Gender Differences
in L2 Learning Strategy Use
Rebecca L. Oxford 1

Gender Equity: Still Knocking at the Classroom Door
David Sadker 27

A Case For Studying Sexism in the ESL Classroom
Mary Yepez 37

Using Inclusive Language in the ESOL Classroom:
The Medusa Syndrome
Effie Papatzikou Cochran 53

Disciplining the Schoolgirl Body
Barbara Kamler 67

Gender and Classroom Research: What's Special about
the Language Classroom?
Jane Sunderland 93

Sexist Language and Instruction in Writing
Michael Newman 121

Gender in Public Life: Pedagogy for ESL
Joan Lesikin and **Alice H. Deakins** 137

Foreword

Issues in Gender, Language Learning,
and
Classroom Pedagogy

Our nation is in the midst of a linguistic tug-of-war, a cultural tussle to define critical words and phrases. The meaning of terms like *political correctness, sexism,* and *advocacy research* are distorted under the weight of ideology. *Affirmative action* is a case in point. While some decry the practice as a distasteful and unfair female and minority preference program, others believe it to be an important counterweight to societal sexism and racism. Few analyze the ideology hidden in the term. For instance, the practice of "legacies" is conveniently omitted from the definition. As a result, few Americans are even aware of the legacy practice by which Ivy League colleges perpetuate the status quo by giving admission breaks to children of their own graduates. The applicants receiving these admission preferences are overwhelmingly white, English speaking, and often wealthy. By calling this practice "legacy" rather than "affirmative action" (in this case, for the privileged), the practice escapes public scrutiny.

Gender is often at the fulcrum of this linguistic cultural clash. For instance, social commentators who criticize male behaviors are ridiculed as "male bashers", dismissed as a somewhat bizarre minority of feminist extremists. Few take time to consider the linguistic irony and social deception concealed in the term "male bashing". Let's face it, damn few women "bash" men. Yet bashing by males is camouflaged in terms like "spousal abuse" or "road rage", phrases which conveniently omit the gender of the perpetrators (who happen to be overwhelmingly male). Such is the political power of language to create bogus realities.

Teachers need to enable their students to analyze these linguistic acrobatics if we are to move beyond them. That's what this book is all about. The intriguing articles in this volume explore the intricacies and intersections of language, multiculturalism, and gender in schools, offering the reader potent insights into how language (mis)shapes reality. Teachers who are intentional about their language are the same instructors who will likely be intentional about their teaching behaviors as well. Thoughtful teachers seek out female students who need this teacher initiative. This book speaks to the importance of teachers investing time and attention to insure that all students, including these quiet ones, participate in class.

Teachers who are thoughtful about what they say are typically thoughtful of how they teach. This book is for them, and for those who hope to be like them.

David Sadker

i

ISSUES IN GENDER, LANGUAGE LEARNING, AND CLASSROOM PEDAGOGY

OVERVIEW

Because gender inequity in education is a global phenomenon affecting all cultures, the collection of articles in this volume is international in its scope and draws on the expertise of scholars / educators from both the United States and abroad. It is vital that teachers, especially teachers of ESOL and EFL, be aware of gender inequities and avoid displaying actively sexist behavior in the classroom. Furthermore, teachers need to promote an inclusive atmosphere so that the students who would otherwise suffer in silence can thrive in a positive learning environment.

Awareness of gender issues has a long history. As far back as the 1930's we find research which identifies sex/gender as a variable worthy of study. In the thirties, enormous attention was paid to sexual behaviors by anthropologists, including Margaret Mead. As one of the first female scientists to travel abroad, Mead, in Sex and Temperament in Three Societies (1935), documented gender-specific behaviors as they emerged from her observations of Pacific Islands communities.

But it was the surge of feminism in the 1970's that gave gender studies its biggest push forward. An enormous upheaval began to take place, radically changing western concepts of male and female roles. Expectations of traditional roles were challenged and communication between the sexes became a source of interest and at times friction. As society's interest in male/female communicative styles increased, works by such authors as Deborah Tannen and Robin Lakoff helped clarify some of the issues that arose from so much sociological change. Tannen's book You Just Don't Understand (1990) has helped demystify some of the characteristics of the verbal war between males and females, particularly in romantic relationships. By pointing out that the sexes have different speech goals (men use language to maintain freedom and social position while females use it to bond and build relationships), she suggests that an understanding of the differences between males and females can help communication. While Lakoff and Tannen were addressing sociological issues, E. Maccoby and C. Jacklin offered us revolutionary information from a cognitive perspective in their work The Psychology of Sex Differences (1974), as did Carol Gilligan in her 1982 book In a Different Voice.

In the 1970's and 1980's gender studies found their way into the field of education, and the impact of male and female interactive behavior in classrooms has now been observed and documented. The effect of such research has been to improve classroom gender dynamics and make educational environments more equitable to women. Again, Tannen, in an article entitled "Teachers' Classroom Strategies Should Recognize that Men and Women Use Language Differently" (1991), sums up some of the more glaring inequities that appear in classrooms and gives remedies for them. These problems had previously been described in depth by Roberta Hall (1982) and others.

But it is the work of Myra and David Sadker that put gender inequity at the forefront of educational concerns, in the same category as socioeconomic and racial issues. In their Gender Equity Handbook (1982), they clearly stated the problems of gender inequity and provided excellent observation instruments for educators. These instruments help educators code their own behavior with male and female students so that they may be sensitized to and, if necessary, change inequitable classroom practices.

While interest in gender inequity in the classroom has been generated at all levels of education (elementary to university) and in all subjects (science, math, etc.), language teachers in particular have begun to focus on these inequities in the language learning classroom. One teacher trainer, Alice Deakins of William Paterson University, began to teach gender and language classes at Columbia University in the early 1980's, sensitizing a generation of language teachers to their treatment of male and female language learners. As her students, Effie Cochran and Mary Yepez became interested in gender interactive behaviors while teaching speakers of other languages.

In the 1980's, Yepez studied ESL teachers in order to ascertain their interaction patterns with male and female English learners. Using the INTERSECT instrument developed by David and Myra Sadker, she documented seven ESL teachers' teaching styles and their own perceptions of their levels of equity with male and female students. It was at this time that the idea to compile a corpus of work on gender and language was conceived by Cochran and Yepez, and the result is the present volume.

This collection of essays begins with Rebecca L. Oxford's article "A Synthesis of Existing Research on Gender Differences in L2 Learning Strategy Use". After offering a synthesis of the research that already exists, including her own original work on the various strategies different language learners use, Oxford reviews findings in learning strategy use from China, Japan, Puerto Rico, South America, and Africa to Western and Eastern Europe, including Russia. David Sadker's article "Gender Equity: Still Knocking at the Classroom Door" summarizes how far we have come since the establishment of Title IX. Both David Sadker's and his late wife, Myra Sadker's research serves as a foundation for much of the work done in gender and education studies. Their extraordinary contribution to this field has helped change many lives. Mary Yepez's essay "A Case for Studying Sexism in the ESL Classroom" encourages English as a Second Language teachers to examine their own interactive behavior with male and female students; it can be used for teacher training. Effie Cochran's article "Using Inclusive Language in the ESOL Classroom: the Medusa Syndrome" describes and explains the petrifying effects that potentially strong and status quo-upsetting women have on men; she coined the phrase "Medusa Syndrome" in the early 80's. Cochran gives a historical perspective and offers practical recommendations to ESOL teachers. From Australia, Barbara Kamler offers us insight into how teachers are powerless to resist the gendering of their own classroom. In her piece "Disciplining the Schoolgirl Body" she shows us, *via* an ethnographic study, how songs and other early childhood pedagogy influence gender-specific pupil selection. Hailing from England, Jane Sunderland, in "Gender and Classroom Research: What's Special About the Language Classroom?", presents research carried out in a foreign language classroom (German). She develops a series of detailed guidelines for those intending to do research in the foreign or additional language classroom in the context of gender issues. Among several interesting conclusions, she hypothesizes that the language classroom may be a female-dominant world, but cautions the reader that -- while language teachers may appear to favor girls -- in reality they may be favoring the higher ability students (who are coincidentally female). Michael Newman, in "Sexist Language and Instruction in Writing", analyzes the prescriptive character of the feminist language critique, showing how complex and subtle both the discerning and the avoiding of sexist language can be. He argues that simplistic, dogmatic assertions in the sexist language debate can be as irrational and judgmental as the prohibitions of traditional prescriptive grammar are. "Sexist *language* is not the issue", he asserts, "sexist *meaning* is, and *sexist* meaning cannot be dealt with by a list of approved and proscribed usages because the forms [by] themselves are not meaningful." Finally, Joan Lesikin and Alice Deakins in "Gender in Public Life: Pedagogy for ESL", contribute a gender-theme curriculum with which English teachers can teach language using high interest topics and can sensitize themselves as well as their students to gender issues and culture. They suggest tasks such as freewriting, inventories, listening, reading and oral prompts, video/role playing activities, and other activities to generate awareness of gender issues as language learning proceeds.

ACKNOWLEDGEMENTS

The editors wish to thank the authors for their contributions to this publication. David Sadker has our gratitude for his allowing us to reprint his powerful article, and for writing the foreword for us. Special thanks go to our mentor Alice Deakins, for her inspirational teaching and for her commitment to gender studies and to Paul Cochran for his constant editorial vigilance. We are also grateful to the New Jersey TESOL-NJBE Board for their interest and support of this volume's publication. Finally, we thank Genaro Bastos whose unfailing support saw the project to its completion.

Effie Papatzikou Cochran
Mary Yepez

A SYNTHESIS OF EXISTING RESEARCH ON GENDER DIFFERENCES IN L2 LEARNING STRATEGY USE

by
Rebecca L. Oxford
University of Maryland

ABSTRACT

This article reviews existing research on gender differences in the use of language learning strategies in many parts of the world. A rather surprising unanimity has surfaced in the majority of studies. The preponderant pattern is for females to use language learning strategies significantly more often than males. However, this typical pattern does not occur everywhere. Certain cultures show that the use of particular types of language learning strategies is greater for males than for females. This article points towards a combination of factors, including socialization and biology, that might influence the situation.

INTRODUCTION

Foreign or second language (L2) learning strategies are specific actions, behaviors, steps, or techniques that students use -- often consciously -- to improve their own progress in internalizing, storing, and using L2 (Oxford 1990a, 1990b, Rigney 1978). Strategies are the tools for active, self-directed involvement that are necessary for developing L2 communicative ability (Wenden & Rubin 1987, O'Malley & Chamot 1990). Illustrations are Suzanne's seeking out conversation partners, Mikhail's grouping and labeling words that are related, Lidia's giving herself encouragement through positive self-talk, Ashraf's using gestures to stay in a conversation when a needed word is unknown, Gustav's learning words by breaking them down into parts, Feng-jie's drawing "semantic maps" with lines and arrows pictorially showing the linkages between new words according to their meaning, and Lazlo's guessing meanings from context. L2 learning strategies like these are very important, because research has repeatedly shown that the conscious, "tailored" use of these strategies is related to language achievement and proficiency (Oxford & Burry 1993, see also Oxford 1989, O'Malley & Chamot 1990, Wenden & Rubin 1987, Cohen 1990, Skehan 1989).

Gender differences appear very frequently in the use of various L2 learning strategies, and in most but not all cases it is the females who report employing such strategies significantly more often than men. The main purpose of this chapter is to synthesize existing research ~ both published and as yet unpublished ~ on gender differences in L2 strategy use. An additional purpose is to provide implications and further questions to consider.

REVIEW OF RELEVANT RESEARCH: This review covers strategies of more and less effective L2 learners and gender differences in strategy choice.

STRATEGIES OF MORE AND LESS EFFECTIVE L2 LEARNERS

Techniques often used for assessing students' L2 strategies include informal observation, formal observational rating scales, informal or formal interviews, group discussions, think-aloud procedures, language learning diaries, dialogue journals between student and teacher, open-ended narrative-type surveys, structured surveys of strategy frequency, and even computer tracking. Results reported in this section and later in this chapter deal largely with survey-based strategy assessment.

Strategies of more effective L2 learners

Early researchers tended to make lists of strategies and other features presumed to be essential for all "good L2 learners". For instance, Rubin (1975) offered the following list of characteristics of such learners:

- **Use guessing willingly and accurately**
- **Have a strong drive to communicate**

- **Are often uninhibited and willing to make mistakes**
- **Focus on form by looking for patterns and analyzing**
- **Take advantage of all practice opportunities**
- **Monitor their own speech and that of others**
- **Pay attention to meaning.**

Naiman, Frohlich, and Todesco (1975) developed a list of strategies used by good L2 learners, adding that these learners learn to think in the language and address the affective aspects of language learning. In 1975 Stern also offered his first set of strategies of good L2 learners, followed by another list in 1983.

L2 research has supported the effectiveness of using L2 learning strategies and has shown that successful language learners typically use strategies in an organized way. Here are some of the main findings:

● *Use of appropriate language learning strategies often results in improved proficiency or achievement overall or in specific skill areas* (see Cohen 1990; Oxford & Crookall 1989; Oxford, Park-Oh, Ito, & Sumrall 1993a, 1993b; Chamot & Kupper 1989; O'Malley & Chamot 1990; Oxford & Burry 1993).

● *Successful language learners tend to select strategies that work well together in a highly orchestrated way,* tailored to the requirements of the language task (Vann & Abraham 1989; Chamot & Kupper 1989).

● *Cognitive strategies (e.g., translating, analyzing, taking notes) and metacognitive strategies (e.g., self-evaluating, planning, organizing) are often used together,* supporting each other (Oxford & Crookall 1989).

● *Social and affective strategies are far less frequently found,* probably because these behaviors are not as carefully studied and also because learners are not familiar with paying attention to their own feelings and social relationships as part of the L2 learning process (Oxford 1990b).

Three points of view exist in studies about strategies of less effective L2 learners. It may be that each one of the three is true for at least some less effective learners. Some of these learners might be very limited in the number and quality of their strategies (Nyikos 1987); others might be unaware of their strategies and thus unable to describe them (Nyikos 1987), and still others might use large numbers of strategies that lack coherence (Vann & Abraham 1989).

• *Gender as an influence on Choice of L2 learning strategies:* According to recent research, gender might be one of the most important influences on the choice of L2 learning strategies (for reviews see Oxford 1993a, 1993b). Other factors include: motivation, cultural background, type of task, age, L2 learning stage, learning style (analytic/global, random /sequential), personality type (extroverted / introverted, intuitive / sensing, thinking / feeling, judging / perceiving), sensory preference (visual / auditory / kinesthetic / tactile), and tolerance of ambiguity (for details, see Oxford 1989).

• *Gender differences in social and linguistic development:* According to hundreds of studies (Maccoby & Jacklin 1974), females show greater interest than males in social activities, prefer "gentle" interaction to aggressive interaction, and are more cooperative and less competitive than males. A meta-analysis by Hyde and Linn (1986) showed substantive gender differences in aggression (both verbal and physical), amounting to .5 standard deviation, with males more aggressive than females. Even in early childhood, girls establish intense, nurturing, empathic relationships in pairs and triads, while boys travel in larger groups characterized by dominance-aggression hierarchies; these patterns continue through adulthood (Maccoby & Jacklin 1974, Gilligan 1982). Females are more likely than males to show continuing need for approval and desire to please others through good grades and social behavior (Mansnerus 1989, Nyikos 1990). They also smile and laugh significantly more than males (Hyde & Linn 1986).

Developmental differences in verbal skill are sometimes very pronounced (Halpern 1986). In the native language (L1), girls usually say their first words and learn to speak in sentences earlier than do boys. This produces an initial "rate advantage" (Larsen-Freeman & Long 1991). Later on, women often speak in longer, more complex sentences than men and score higher than men on tests of spelling, grammar, and perceptual speed. Boys have a far greater frequency of disabilities in learning, reading, and speaking than do girls. On verbal ability tests and reading tests females on the average surpass males, particularly from age 11 on, according to most studies (Cahn 1988, Gage & Berliner 1975, Maccoby & Jacklin 1974, Slavin 1988). However, a few studies show a slight, temporary drop in standardized verbal tests among girls during adolescence, possibly because of the recent inclusion of scientific and business topics (Nyikos 1990, Mansnerus 1989) or because of gender-related peer pressure against performing optimally.

Compared with men's L1 or native speech, women's L1 speech in many parts of the world shows more empathy, concern, politeness, encouragement of other speakers, negotiation, detail-remembering, uncertainty, questioning behavior, and grammaticality (Lakoff 1975, Tannen 1986, 1990, Kramarae 1981). Men use more verbal expressions of power and aggression, adversarial-argumentative style, interruption, ridicule, analytical critique, and discouragement of other speakers (Belenky, Clinchy, Goldberger, & Tarule 1986, Tannen 1986, 1990). Anthropologists Brown and Levinson and sociologists Giles and Tajfel attribute such L1 differences to socialization, with special reference to the subordinate role of women in economic and political spheres (for details, see Kramarae 1981, Thorne, Kramarae, and Henley 1983).

Gass and Varonis (1986) studied the conversational behavior of L2 learners. Men dominated conversations, but women initiated more "negotiations of meaning", trying to understand and communicate clearly. In learning an L2, males and females sometimes show different levels of skill, especially in listening. Eisenstein (1982) found that females surpassed males on listening tasks which involved discriminating among dialects and recognizing dialects that had various degrees of social prestige. Likewise, Farhady (1982), with a sample of 800 university students, discovered that females outperformed males in the area of listening comprehension.

•   *Gender differences in strategy use of native English speakers learning other languages:* Table 1 shows the statistically significant results of studies of gender differences in L2 strategy use for native speakers of English learning other languages.

TABLE 1

**Significant gender differences in strategy use
of native speakers of English learning other languages**

Date	Researcher	Languages learned	Females use more strategies than males	Males use more strategies than females
1983	Politzer	French, German, Spanish	- Social strategies	None
1988	Ehrman & Oxford	Many	- General study - Negotiating meaning - Functional practice - Self-management	None
1989	Oxford & Nyikos	French, German, Spanish, Italian, Russian	- Formal rule-based strategies - General study strategies - Conversational input-elicitation strategies	None
1987	Nyikos	German	**After strategy training:** - Color only memory strategies	**After strategy training:** - Color-plus-picture strategies
1993	Oxford, Park-Oh, & Ito	Japanese	- Cognitive strategies	None
1993	Sumrall	Japanese	- Social strategies - Affective strategies	None

TABLE 1
(continued)

**Significant gender differences in strategy use
of native speakers of English learning other languages**

Date	Researcher	Languages learned	Females use more strategies than males	Males use more strategies than females

1996	Oxford, Lavine, Felkins, Hollaway, & Saleh	Spanish	- Cognitive strategies
			- Memory strategies
			- Social strategies
			- Affective strategies
			- **Specific strategies:**
			  . *Trying out new vocabulary learning techniques*
			  . *Judging success of a particular strategy*
				None
				
				- **Specific strategies:**
				  . *Thinking about my progress*

1990 & 1991	Brecht, Davidson, & Ginsberg	Russian (in Russia)	- Social strategies - Affective strategies	None

1995	Zoubir-Shaw & Oxford	French	- **Strategies catagories:**
			  . *Learning conjugations*
			  . *Learning grammar structure rules*
			  . *Learning from context*
			- **Specific strategies:**
			  . *Using color-coded cards for gender*
			  . *Using pink & blue for gender*
			  . *Using other color for gender*
			  . *Using flash cards*
			  . *Using lists organized in grammatical classes*
			  . *Accepting rules at face value*
			  . *Reviewing from text material*
				- **Strategies catagories:**
				  . *Learning from various activities*
				
				- **Specific strategies:**
				  . *Concentrating more on oral communication than structure*
				  . *Being impaired by not knowing the meaning of a word (negative strategy)*
				  . *Review from test material only (negative strategy)*
				  . *Looking for general meaning idea, or theme*

1995	Oxford & Ehrman	Multiple languages	- Compensation strategies	None

Oxford, Nyikos, and Ehrman (1988) were the first to publish a review of studies involving gender differences in L2 learning strategies. At that time, out of a selection of over 80 investigations of L2 learning strategies, only four mentioned gender differences at all. Since that time, more research has been done on this topic.

The first of the four studies described in the 1988 review was by Politzer (1983), who employed his own strategy inventory with 90 American students learning French, Spanish, or German. Politzer reported that female college students used social strategies for L2 learning significantly more often than their male peers – a difference which he did not explain but which might be related to gender differences in social orientation.

In another study discussed in the 1988 review, Ehrman and Oxford (1989) used the Strategy Inventory for Language Learning (published in Oxford 1990b) with 79 adults in an intensive foreign language learning setting, the Foreign Service Institute of the U.S. Department of State. The range of languages learned was very large. Those authors found that females, compared with males, reported significantly greater use of L2 learning strategies in four factor-analytically derived categories: general study strategies, strategies for negotiating meaning, self-management strategies, and functional practice strategies.

Another study in the 1988 review was by Oxford and Nyikos and was published the next year (1989). The researchers used the Strategy Inventory for Language Learning with 1,200 university students, each of whom was learning one or more of these languages: French, Spanish, German, Russian, and Italian. These investigators found that female students, contrasted with males, used L2 learning strategies significantly more often in three of five factor-analytically derived categories: formal rule-based strategies, general study strategies, and conversational input-elicitation strategies. The gender differences found in the second and third studies might be associated with women's social skills, stronger verbal skills (including pattern usage), and greater conformity to academic and linguistic norms.

The final study in the 1988 review was by Nyikos (1987), who discovered significant gender differences among 135 university students in using memory strategies for German vocabulary learning. Nyikos used her own strategy assessment instrument for this study. After training in the use of these strategies, men outperformed women in the color-plus-picture combination, which was explained as potentially related to men's putatively greater visual-spatial acuity. However, women surpassed men in the color-only condition, which was explained by women's greater interest in color (often as a social attractor).

Using an L2 learning strategy survey oriented toward distance education and adapted from the Strategy Inventory for Language Learning, Oxford, Park-Oh, Ito, and Sumrall (1993a, 1993b) discovered gender-difference trends among 107 high school students studying Japanese by satellite. Females tended to use many cognitive strategies, social strategies, and affective (emotion-related) strategies more often than males. Gender differences were not as strong in metacognitive, compensation, and memory strategies. Males in this study, as in others, did not surpass females in strategy use in any of the main strategy categories. Females also outperformed males in terms of motivation and Japanese language achievement.

Lavine and Oxford (see Oxford, Lavine, Felkins, Hollaway, & Saleh 1986) found gender differences in learning strategy use via the diaries of 42 Spanish language students at the university level. Several of the general strategy-category differences favored women and none favored men. For instance, significantly more females than males used cognitive, memory, social, and affective strategies, though the percentage differences were not large. In terms of specific strategies rather than overall categories, the strategy of trying out new techniques for vocabulary learning was used significantly more often by women than men. However, some gender differences favoring males were seen for specific strategies. For instance, more men than women used self-evaluating across the three skills of listening comprehension, grammar, and vocabulary, and in vocabulary learning, men surpassed women in using the strategy of judging the success of a particular strategy. Lavine and Oxford suggested that these differences might relate to female and male "ways of knowing", with women focused more on the process and on alternative solutions and men centered more on outcomes.

In the only research conducted on informal language development of American students in the target country, Brecht, Davidson, and Ginsberg (1990, 1991) found some of the expected gender differences to be reversed. American male college students on study-abroad programs in Russia (hence Russian as a second language) were more likely to improve their proficiency, more likely to use social and affective strategies, and more likely to employ a broader range of strategies than women. Brecht *et al.* suggest that the greater aggression of the male students allowed them greater access to the foreign culture, thus providing them with more opportunities to develop types of strategies beyond those they would typically use in the classroom.

Zoubir-Shaw and Oxford (1995) used the Romance Language Learning Strategy Survey to assess the strategy use of 25 university-level students of introductory French. Four of the nine strategy categories on the survey exhibited gender differences. Three of these (strategies for learning conjugations, strategies for learning grammar structures/rules, and strategies for learning from context) favored females as more frequent strategy users, while the fourth (strategies for learning from various activities) showed greater strategy use by males. When separate strategies were considered, women surpassed men in 7 of the 12 strategies for which gender differences were found. Women more frequently than men used strategies involving visual details (color coding and flashcards), reviewing, and contextualized learning. Three of the five strategies which men used significantly more often than women were negative, such as failing to compare and accept rules as part of a separate system, becoming impaired when a word's meaning is not known, and reviewing only from previous test material. Other male-dominant strategies were concentrating more on oral communication than on structures and looking for the main idea or theme, underscoring a surprisingly global language learning approach for the men in this sample.

Oxford and Ehrman (1995) studied the learning strategies and other characteristics of a highly selective group of 268 adult learners, primarily native English speakers, who were learning foreign languages at the U.S. Foreign Service Institute. Many of these learners were already diplomats or were headed toward careers in foreign diplomacy. In this group, women scored higher on overall strategy use (the average of all the subscales on the Strategy Inventory for Language Learning). Compared with men, women also showed significantly more frequent use of compensation strategies to make up for missing knowledge.

Gender differences in strategy use of learners of English as a second or foreign language.

(Table 2 illustrates statistically significant gender differences in strategy use among learners of ESL or EFL around the world.)

TABLE 2

**Significant gender differences in strategy use
of non-native speakers of English
learning English as a second or foreign language**

Date	Researcher	ESL vs. EFL	Females use more strategies than males	Males use more strategies than females
1988	Tran	ESL Vietnamese	- Not cited	- In general
1988	Willing	ESL Mixed	- Learning many new words - Learning by seeing - Learning by doing - Learning by talking to friends	- Writing in notebook - Learning by cassettes
1993	Bedell	EFL Chinese	- Factor-analytic: . *Compensation strategies* . *Memory strategies* - Metacognitive strategies . *Organizing a notebook* . *Reading several times* . *Skimming then reading* . *Concentrating on speaker* . *Revising a written piece*	- Factor-analytic: . *Functional practice-production strategies* - Formal/ affective strategies . *Applying general rules* . *Finding practice opportunities*

(Table # 2 Continued)

Date	Researcher	ESL vs. EFL	Females use more strategies than males	Males use more strategies than females
1992	Yang	EFL Chinese	- Social strategies	- None
1991	Chang	EFL Chinese	- None	- None
1991	Noguchi	EFL Japanese	- **Metacognitive strategies:** . *In general*	- None
1991	Green	ESL/EFL Puerto Rican	- **Metacognitive strategies:** . *Social strategies*	- None
1995	Green & Oxford	ESL/EFL Puerto Rican	- Memory strategies - **Metacognitive strategies:** . *Affective strategies* . *Social Strategies* - **Specific strategies:** . Using flash cards . Reviewing often . Learning words by location . Skimming then reading . Making summaries . Using gestures . Trying to find out about language learning process . Thinking about my progress . Giving myself a reward . Noticing my tension . Asking for slower speech or repetition . Asking for correction . Asking for help	- None - **Specific strategies:** . Watching TV or movies in English
1994	Salies	EFL Brazilian	- In general - Affective strategies	- Memory
1996	Dreyer & Oxford	ESL Afrikaans	- Social strategies - Metacognitive strategies	- None

(Table # 2 Continued)

Date	Researcher	ESL vs. EFL	Females use more strategies than males	Males use more strategies than females
1996	Kaylani	EFL Jordanian	- Memory strategies - Cognitive strategies - Affective strategies	- None
1996	Dadour & Robbins	EFL Egyptian	- None	- None
1997	Mathias	EFL Belgian	- In general	- None
1999	Sheorey	EFL Indian	- In general - Cognitive-memory - Metacognitive - Social	- None
Undated	Frumina, Khasan, & Leaver	EFL Russian	(General stream:) - Memory - Cognitive - Metacognitive - Affective - Social	- None
Undated	Frumina, Khasan, & Leaver	EFL Russian	(Advanced stream:) - Memory - Cognitive - Metacognitive - Compensation - Affective	- None

Tran (1988), using his own strategy assessment instrument, studied gender differences in English language acculturation and learning strategies among Vietnamese adults over 40 in the U.S. He found that females had more L2 learning problems and that males were more likely than females to use a variety of L2 learning strategies to improve their English skills. Possibly age and cultural gender-role differences influenced these results.

In a study of 500 ESL learners in Australia employing his own strategy assessment tool, Willing (1988) discovered interesting gender differences in L2 learning strategies. Significant differences included the following. Women more often than men indicated they liked to learn many new words, to learn English words by seeing them, to learn English words by "doing something", and to learn by talking to friends in English. Although the following two strategies were not favored by either males or females to a high degree, men more often than women said they wanted to write everything in their notebooks and liked to learn by using cassettes. Thus, more of the significant differences in strategy choice favored females.

Bedell (1993) used the Strategy Inventory for Language Learning, translated into Chinese, with a sample of 353 mostly high-achieving EFL students from several mainland Chinese postsecondary institutions to determine language learning strategy use. The overall mean was slightly, but non-significantly, higher for females than males. Bedell found that 17 strategies showed significant gender differences, 15 favoring greater usage by females and the other two by males. Several of the "female strategies" were those requiring patience and attention to detail: organizing a notebook, reading a story several times, skimming and then rereading, concentrating while someone else is speaking, and revising a written piece. Women in China, according to Bedell, might be better socialized than males for these kinds of tasks. The only "male strategies" were applying general rules to new situations and finding opportunities to practice English. Examining the survey's six parts or strategy categories, Bedell found that females were significantly more likely than males to use compensation strategies and memory strategies; no significant gender differences favored males as strategy users in this analysis. The picture was somewhat different when Bedell contrasted males and females on the nine factors from his own Varimax factor analysis. Females significantly surpassed males in the use of compensation strategies (factor 3), memory strategies (factors 5 and 6), and metacognitive strategies (factor 2). Men did not score higher than women on many of the factors, but for those factors on which they did score higher, the difference was strong: functional practice-productive strategies (factor 1) and formal practice and affective strategies (factor 7).

Yang (1992, 1993) used a Chinese translation of the Strategy Inventory for Language Learning with 505 Taiwanese EFL students, mostly in their first year of university studies. She discovered significantly higher use of social strategies among the women compared with the men.

Chang (1991) was the only researcher studying strategy use of Chinese students who did not find any significant gender differences. Using a Chinese translation of the Strategy Inventory for Language Learning with 50 mainland and Taiwanese students who were studying ESL at the University of Georgia, Chang found that gender did not influence strategy use.

Noguchi (1991) used a Japanese language strategy survey derived from the Strategy Inventory for Language Learning to assess the learning strategy use of 174 junior high students learning third-year EFL. Overall, Noguchi found that girls used language learning strategies more often than boys in this sample.

Green (1991) used the Strategy Inventory for Language Learning with 213 prebasic, basic, and intermediate English students at the University of Puerto Rico in Mayaguez. This can be considered a "hybrid" ESL/EFL environment. Like ESL students the Puerto Ricans have strong English input all around them, but like EFL students they do not have to use English for daily survival. In terms of strategy categories, females surpassed males in metacognitive and social strategy use; males did not use any strategy category more often than females.

In a larger study with the same instrument at the same university, Green and Oxford (1995) studied the strategy use of 374 prebasic, basic, and intermediate English students. Memory, metacognitive, affective, and social strategies were used significantly more often by women than men. Cognitive and compensation strategies showed no significant gender differences. Specific strategies used more often by women were using flash cards, reviewing often, learning words by location, skimming first then reading, making summaries, using gestures, trying to find out about language learning processes, thinking about one's own progress, giving oneself a reward, noticing tension, asking for slower speech or repetition, asking for correction, and asking for help. The only strategy that men used significantly more than women was watching TV or movies in English.

Salies (1994) studied patterns of learning strategies of 315 teenage and adult students of EFL in Brazil. The Strategy Inventory for Language Learning was employed. Females reported a higher frequency of overall use of strategies in this study, although males showed a higher frequency of memory and affective strategies.

Examining 305 South African university EFL students whose native language is Afrikaans, Dreyer and Oxford (1996) found significant differences between males and females in strategy use on the Strategy Inventory for Language Learning. A significant gender difference in overall use of learning strategies was identified between males and females, with females having the higher average strategy use. Females showed significantly more frequent use of most strategy groups, especially the categories of social and metacognitive strategies.

In a study of EFL learners in Jordan, Kaylani (1996) discovered that both gender and motivation were related to strategy frequencies of 255 high school seniors. Differences in strategy use were found for memory, compensation, cognitive, and affective strategies, with females surpassing males in strategy use. However, there was no significant gender difference in social strategy use, primarily because (as Kaylani explained) females are frequently prohibited from speaking in public, particularly when males are present. In this study, females and males showed different patterns of motivation for language learning, with males being more "integratively motivated" to become part of the culture and females being more "instrumentally motivated" to learn English to succeed at the university (and therefore in marriage prospects).

Another Middle Eastern study was conducted, this time in Egypt by Dadour (see Dadour & Robbins 1996). This study involved 122 first- and fourth-year university students of EFL. Males and females did not differ significantly in their array of chosen learning strategies as measured by the Strategy Inventory for Language Learning. However, males performed better than females in oral communication, a result explained because males had greater cultural opportunities and encouragement to use the language.

Mathias (1997) conducted a study of EFL strategy use among 52 adult students enrolled at a theological seminary in Belgium. They represented a number of native language groups: French, Finnish, German, Swedish, Afrikaans, Bulgarian, Chinese, Italian, Kisongye, Lingala, Portuguese, and Twi. Compared with males, females in the study showed significantly higher levels of greater overall strategy use on the Strategy Inventory for Language Learning.

Sheorey (1999) used an adapted version of the Strategy Inventory for Language Learning, known as the English Language Learning Strategies Inventory, to assess the strategy use of 1,261 Indian college students studying EFL in the environment of an indigenized, vernacular variety of English. Females in this study reported significantly more frequent use of strategies than males, just as did students whose English proficiency was high. Females reported significantly greater use of strategies in three of four strategy categories: cognitive-memory, metacognitive, and social strategies. Only the means for functional practice strategies showed no gender differences. Females' mean for 21 of the 33 strategy items was significantly higher than that for male students.

Frumina, Khasan, and Leaver (undated) examined the learning strategies of 152 university-level Russian students learning EFL. These students were in two "streams": the general stream and the International Baccalaureate stream (the latter being more accelerated and advanced). Within the general stream, significant gender differences repeatedly occurred for five out of six strategy categories, in each case with women surpassing men in strategy use: memory, cognitive, metacognitive, affective, and social. In the IB stream, however, the pattern was slightly different. IB women used strategies more frequently than men in the categories of memory, metacognitive, and affective strategies, but IB men used cognitive and compensation strategies more often than women.

Possible causes of these gender differences. Socialization is one of the main causes of many of these gender differences (Crawford & Gentry 1989, Dadour & Robbins 1996, Dunn 1991, Eccles 1989, Jacklin 1983, Kaylani 1996, Nyikos 1990, Sheorey 1999, Slavin 1988). As Bedell (1993) noted, some gender differences are to be expected across cultures. One model cited by Bedell suggests that some cultures, like Japan and Mexico, have sharply defined gender roles (which could imply strong gender differences in learning), while others, like Scandinavia and Costa Rica, have more overlapping gender roles (implying weak gender differences in learning), and Chinese culture has moderately defined gender roles (implying moderate gender differences in learning). In some cultures, the male role is socially dominant, thus causing certain direct or indirect repercussions for strategy use (Dadour & Robbins 1996, Kaylani 1996, Sheorey 1999).

However, Moir and Jessel (1991) argue that "brain sex" (anatomical difference in heterosexual male and female brains) causes some of the observed differences. Gender differences in brain lateralization/hemisphericity have been noted, with greater nerve linkages in the corpus callosum between right and left hemispheres for females than males (Springer & Deutsch 1989) and for homosexual males than heterosexual males (Elias 1992, Associated Press 1992). Furthermore, verbal functioning was found by Kimura (1985) to be more diffuse in women than in men, probably a sign of hemispheric differences. Probably any gender differences arise from an intricate, not fully understood interaction of socialization and physiology.

IMPLICATIONS AND MORE QUESTIONS

As we have seen, a large number of investigations (though not all) demonstrated that females used many language learning strategies more frequently than males. In these studies, not all males learned in the same way, and not all females learned in the same way. Yet there were so many significant differences that we must consider the question: What does this mean for instruction in foreign and second languages?

The first implication for teachers is that knowing how our students function can help us tailor instruction for them. Knowing how both genders learn can help us improve our teaching by causing us to develop workable instructional strategies for both groups. Strategy assessment instruments such as surveys, diaries, observations, think-aloud procedures, and interviews might have great value. The question arises: Which strategy assessment tool is the best for my students? How much information do I need about my students' strategies? How much information do the students need about their own strategies? What strategy assessment mode provides what is necessary without taking too much time? Often the answer is that a survey provides the first and most comprehensive look at strategy use. After that, almost any other tool could be a useful supplement.

The second implication is that we can teach our students, female and male, to use more and better strategies (for details on strategy training, see Oxford 1990b, Oxford & Leaver 1996, Cohen 1998). We should optimize the strategies that males and females use aptly and well, and we should encourage everyone to develop strategies that go beyond gender boundaries. If continued research shows that males or females need help in certain strategies, we can easily teach useful strategies by weaving them into normal lessons. Any student can learn to compensate for strategy weaknesses and can build a larger repertoire of strategies. Questions remain: How far can students stretch themselves and compensate by learning new strategies? What is the best mode for strategy training?

A third implication is that teachers need training to adapt themselves to the students' strategies and learning needs. The teacher needs to know what his or her own general learning styles and specific learning strategies are. To become the best facilitator of learning possible, the teacher can discover the strategies he or she is sharing with the students and can consciously expand this strategy range. We might ask: Can and should teachers discuss their own styles and strategies with their students? To what degree can teachers train students to use strategies that are not traditionally in the teachers' own favored set of techniques?

A fourth implication deals with textbooks. We can start to consider who writes our language textbooks and what strategies these authors include. We can ask these questions: Do the authors purposefully target a wide range of strategies that work with all four language skills? Do they consider the strategy needs of both females and males? Do the strategies in their textbooks consciously or unconsciously reflect one gender? Would it make a difference writing a textbook if the author had both males and females in mind?

A last implication concerns causes of gender differences in strategy use. We can easily see influences of socialization ~ especially educational and family effects ~ on language learning strategy use. Certainly socialization appears to play a powerful role, but brain hemisphericity (roughly reflecting an analytic vs. global contrast) might also have an influence. We might ask: What is the role of the corpus callosum in movement of information between the two hemispheres of the brain, and how does this differ by gender? Is it true that females in general have a thicker corpus callosum than males, allowing more interchange between the two halves of the brain? Does this help create greater flexibility in language learning? Why do females often surpass males in ability to learn foreign languages and in native language achievement as well? Does this relate to hemisphericity? What about some autistic people who have almost no corpus callosum and whose creative language ability is diminished? From an instructional viewpoint, is strategy training a possibility for helping integrate the work of the two hemispheres in normally functioning people? If so, what would be the best age and stage for this to occur?

Many tantalizing questions have been raised about gender differences in L2 strategy use. This paper has shared the most recent findings from relevant research. More studies are needed to answer the remaining questions.

ABOUT THE AUTHOR

Rebecca L. Oxford is a noted author of a number of books on language learning strategies, motivation, and instructional methodology. She has presented keynote speeches at conferences for teachers and researchers on most continents of the world. Among her research interests is the issue of gender in language use and language learning. She holds a Ph.D. in educational psychology from the University of North Carolina, master's degrees from Yale University (Russian language) and Boston University (educational psychology), and a bachelor's degree (Russian language and history) from Vanderbilt University.

REFERENCES

Associated Press. (1992). Study shows brains differ in gay, heterosexual men: Anterior commissure area larger in homosexuals. The Washington Post A2.

Bedell, D. (1993). Crosscultural variation in the choice of language learning strategies: A mainland Chinese investigation with comparison to previous studies. Unpublished master's thesis, University of Alabama, Tuscaloosa, AL.

Belenky, M.F., Clinchy, B.M., Goldberger, N.R., & Tarule, J.M. (1986). Women's ways of knowing: The development of self, voice, and mind. New York: Basic Books.

Brecht, R., Davidson, D., & Ginsberg, R. (1990). The empirical study of proficiency gain in study abroad environments among American students of Russian. In D. Davidson (ed.), American contributions to the VII International Congress of MAPRIAL. Washington, DC: American Council of Teachers of Russian.

Brecht, R., Davidson, D., & Ginsberg, R. (1991). On evaluating language proficiency gain in study abroad environments: An empirical study of American students of Russian (a preliminary analysis of data). In Z. D. Dabars (ed.), Selected papers delivered at the NEH symposium in Russian language and culture. Baltimore: CORLAC/Friends School of Baltimore.

Cahn, L.D. (1988). Sex and grade differences and learning rate in an intensive summer reading clinic. Psychology in the Schools 25(1), 84-91.

Chamot A.U. & Kupper, L. (1989). Learning strategies in foreign language instruction. Foreign Language Annals. 22(1), 13-24.

Chang, S.J. (1991). A study of language learning behaviors of Chinese students at the University of Georgia and the relation of those behaviors to oral proficiency and other factors. Unpublished doctoral dissertation, University of Georgia, Athens, GA.

Cohen, A.D. (1990). Language learning: Insights for learners, teachers, and researchers. New York: Newbury House / Harper & Row.

Cohen, A.D. (1998). Strategies in learning and using a second language. Essex, U.K.: Addison Wesley Longman.

Crawford, M. & Gentry, M., (eds. 1989). Gender and thought: Psychological perspectives. New York: Springer-Verlag.

Dadour, E.S. & Robbins, J. (1996). University-level studies using strategy instruction to improve speaking ability in Egypt and Japan. In R.L. Oxford (Ed.), Language learning strategies around the world: Crosscultural perspectives (pp. 157-166). Manoa: University of Hawaii Press.

Dreyer, C. & Oxford, R. (1996). Learning strategies and other predictors of ESL proficiency among Afrikaans speakers in South Africa. In R.L. Oxford (Ed.), Language learning strategies: Crosscultural perspectives (pp. 61-74). Manoa: University of Hawaii Press.

Dunn, R. (1991). Do students from different cultures have different learning styles? InterEd 15, 12-16.

Eccles, J.S. (1989). Bringing young women to math and science. In M. Crawford & M. Gentry (eds.), Gender and thought: Psychological perspectives (pp. 36-58). New York: Springer-Verlag.

Ehrman, M.E. & Oxford, R.L. (1989). Effects of sex differences, career choice, and psychological type on adults' language learning strategies. Modern Language Journal 73, 1-13.

Eisenstein, M. (1982). A study of social variation in adult second language acquisition. Language Learning 32, 367-391.

Elias, M. (1992, Aug. 3). Difference seen in brains of gay men. USA Today 8D.

Farhady, H. (1982). Measures of language proficiency from the learner's perspective. TESOL Quarterly 16, 43-59.

Frumina, Y., Khasan, B., & Leaver, B.L. (undated). Conflicted and tolerant educational mind-sets and language learning strategies. Salinas, CA: American Global Studies Institute.

Gage, N.L. & Berliner, D.C. (1975). Educational psychology. Chicago: Rand-McNally.

Gass, S. & Varonis, E. (1986). Sex differences in NNS/NNS interactions. In R. Day (ed.), Talking to learn: Conversation in second language acquisition (pp. 327-351). Rowley, MA: Newbury House.

Gilligan, C. (1982). In a different voice: Psychological theory and women's development. Cambridge: Harvard University Press.

Green, J.M. (1991). Language learning strategies of Puerto Rican university students. Paper presented at the annual meeting of Puerto Rico Teachers of English to Speakers of Other Languages, San Juan.

Green, J.M. & Oxford, R.L. (1995). A closer look at learning strategies, L2 proficiency, and gender. TESOL Quarterly, 29 (2), 261-297.

Halpern, D.F. (1986). Sex differences in cognitive abilities. Hillsdale, NJ: Erlbaum.

Hyde, J. & Linn, M.C., eds. (1986). The psychology of gender: Advances through meta-analysis. Baltimore: Johns Hopkins University Press.

Jacklin, C.N. (1983). Boys and girls entering school. In M. Marland (ed.)., Sex differentiation and schooling. London: Heinemann.

Kaylani, C. (1996). Influence of gender and motivation on EFL learning strategy use. In R.L. Oxford (Ed.), Language learning strategies around the world: Crosscultural perspectives (pp. 75-88). Manoa: University of Hawaii Press.

Kimura, D. (1985). Left brain, right brain: The hidden differences. Psychology Today, 85.

Kramarae, C. (1981). Women and men speaking. Rowley, MA: Newbury House.

Lakoff, R. (1975). Language and women's place. New York: Harper & Row.

Larsen-Freeman, D. & Long, M. (1991). An introduction to second language acquisition research. London: Longman.

Maccoby, E.E. & Jacklin, C.N. (1974). The psychology of sex differences. Stanford: Stanford University Press.

Mansnerus, L. (1989, Aug. 6). SAT separates girls from boys. New York Times Sec. 4A, 27-28.

Mathias, M.A. (1997). What SAS says about SILL: A correlational study between learning style and language learning strategies. Thesis, Katholieke Universiteit Leuven, Belgium.

Moir, A. & Jessel, D. (1991). Brain sex: The real difference between men and women. New York: Stuart/Carol.

Naiman, N., Frohlich, M. & Todesco, A. (1975). The good second language learner. TESL Talk. 6(1), 58-75.

Noguchi, T. (1991). Review of language learning strategy research and its implications. Unpublished bachelor's thesis, Tottori University, Tottori, Japan.

Nyikos, M. (1987). The effect of color and imagery as mnemonic strategies on learning and retention of lexical items in German. Dissertation, Purdue University, West Lafayette, IN.

Nyikos, M. (1990). Sex-related differences in adult language learning: Socialization and memory factors. Modern Language Journal 74(3), 273-287.

O'Malley, J.M. & Chamot, A.U. (1990). Learning strategies in second language acquisition. Cambridge: Cambridge University Press.

Oxford, R.L. (1989). Use of language learning strategies: A synthesis of studies with implications for strategy training. System 17, 235-247.

Oxford, R.L. (1990a). Language learning strategies and beyond: A look at strategies in the context of styles. In S.S. Magnan (ed.), Shifting the instructional focus to the learner (pp. 35-55). Middlebury, VT: Northeast Conference on the Teaching of Foreign Languages.

Oxford, R.L. (1990b). Language learning strategies: What every teacher should know. New York: Newbury House / Harper & Row. Now Boston: Heinle & Heinle.

Oxford, R.L. (1993a). Instructional implications of gender differences in L2 learning styles and strategies. Applied Language Learning 4(1-2), 65-94.

Oxford, R.L. (1993b). La différence continue...: Gender differences in second/foreign language learning styles and strategies. In J. Sunderland (ed.), Exploring Gender (pp. 140-147). Englewood Cliffs, NJ: Prentice-Hall.

Oxford, R.L. & Burry, J.A. (1993). Evolution, norming, and psychometric testing of Oxford's Strategy Inventory for Language Learning. Paper presented at the annual meeting of the National Council on Measurement in Education, Atlanta, GA.

Oxford, R.L. & Crookall, D. (1989). Language learning strategies: Methods, findings, and instructional implications. Modern Language Journal 73, 404-419.

Oxford, R.L. & Ehrman, M.E. (1995). Adults' language learning strategies in an intensive foreign language program in the United States. System, 23 (3), 359-386.

Oxford, R.L., Lavine, R.Z., Felkins, G., Hollaway, M.E., & Saleh, A. (1996). Telling their stories: Language students use diaries and recollection. In R.L. Oxford (Ed.), Language learning strategies around the world: Crosscultural perspectives (pp. 19-34). Manoa: University of Hawaii Press.

Oxford, R.L. & Leaver, B.L. (1996). A synthesis of strategy instruction for language learners. In R.L. Oxford (Ed.), Language learning strategies around the world: Crosscultural perspectives (pp.227-246). Manoa: University of Hawaii Press.

Oxford, R.L. & Nyikos, M. (1989). Variables affecting choice of language learning strategies by university students. Modern Language Journal 73, 219-300.

Oxford, R.L., Nyikos, M. & Ehrman, M. (1988). Vive la différence? Reflections on sex differences in use of language learning strategies. Foreign Language Annals 21(4), 321-329.

Oxford, R.L., Park-Oh, Y., Ito, S. & Sumrall, M. (1993a). Factors affecting achievement in a satellite-delivered Japanese language program. American Journal of Distance Education 7(1), 10-25.

Oxford, R.L., Park-Oh, Y., Ito, S. & Sumrall, M. (1993b). Learning Japanese by satellite: What influences student achievement? System 21(1), 31-48.

Politzer, R.L. (1983). An exploratory study of self-reported language learning behaviors and their relation to achievement. Studies in Second Language Acquisition 6, 54-68.

Rigney, J. W. (1978). Learning strategies: A theoretical perspective. In H.F. O'Neil, Jr. (ed.), Learning Strategies (pp. 165-285). New York: Academic Press.

Rubin, J. (1975). What the "good language learner" can teach us. TESOL Quarterly. 9(1), 41-51.

Salies, T.M.G. (1994). Patterns of learning strategies of EFL students: The case of Brazil. Thesis, Oklahoma State University, Stillwater, OK.

Sheorey, R. (1999). An examination of language learning strategy use in the setting of an indigenized variety of English. Paper submitted for publication.

Skehan, P. (1989). Individual differences in second-language learning. London: Edward Arnold.

Slavin, R.E. (1988). Educational psychology: Theory into practice. (2nd ed.), Englewood Cliffs, NJ: Prentice-Hall.

Springer, S. & Deutsch, G. (1989). Left brain, right brain. New York: Freeman.

Stern, H.H. (1975). What can we learn from the good language learner? Canadian Modern Language Review. 31, 304-318.

Stern, H.H. (1983). Fundamental concepts in language teaching. Oxford: Oxford University Press.

Tannen, D. (1986). That's not what I meant! New York: Morrow.

Tannen, D. (1990). You just don't understand: Women and men in conversation. New York: Ballentine.

Thorne, B., Kramarae, C. & Henley, N. (1983). Language, gender, and society. Rowley, MA: Newbury House.

Tran, T.V. (1988). Sex differences in English language acculturation and learning strategies among Vietnamese adults age 40 and over in the United States. Sex Roles 19(11-12), 747-758.

Vann, R. & Abraham, R. (1989). Strategies of unsuccessful language learners. Paper presented at the annual meeting of Teachers of English to Speakers of Other Languages. San Francisco, CA.

Wenden, A. & Rubin, J. (eds.) (1987). Learner strategies for language learning. Englewood Cliffs, NJ: Prentice-Hall.

Willing, K. (1988). Learning styles in adult migrant education. Adelaide, S. Australia: National Curriculum Research Council.

Yang, N.D. (1992). Second language learners' beliefs about language learning and their use of learning strategies: A study of college students of English in Taiwan. Unpublished doctoral dissertation, University of Texas, Austin, TX.

Yang, N.D. (1993). Understanding Chinese students' language beliefs and learning strategy use. Paper presented at the annual meeting of International Teachers of English to Speakers of Other Languages, Atlanta, GA.

Zoubir-Shaw, S. & Oxford, R.L. (1995). Gender differences in language learning strategy use in university-level introductory French classes: A pilot study using a strategy questionnaire. In C. Klee (Ed.), Faces in a crowd: Individual learners in multisection courses (pp. 181-213). Boston: Heinle & Heinle.

GENDER EQUITY:
STILL KNOCKING AT THE CLASSROOM DOOR

by
David Sadker
American University, Washington, DC

ABSTRACT

Gender equity? Oh, yes, that was big a few years ago. Today, girls' home economics and boys' shop are gone.

Girls get better grades. Girls are more likely to get into college whereas boys are more likely to get into trouble. Why all this attention to girls? Boys are the ones in trouble.

This article discusses research showing that despite feminist gains of the last forty years, gender equity remains an unfulfilled goal. In spite of the conservative media's prevailing efforts to convince the larger society that there is no gender bias (except that against men), educators never cease to surprise themselves when they discover their own subtle "gender blindness" on videotape. The article asserts that creating single-gender classes and schools is a false solution to the need for egalitarian public education. Ten gender-bias updates are also outlined.

TITLE IX? WASN'T THAT REPEALED?

Many educators are confused about gender equity. Is it still a problem? Is it more about political correctness than about educational effectiveness? Wasn't that battle fought and won years ago? Through the 1970's, Ivy League schools such as Columbia University did not even admit women. Today, the majority of college students are women. Perhaps we should declare victory and move on.

Michael Kazin, in his forthcoming book *Like a Civil War: The United States in the 1960s* (Oxford University Press, in press), helps educators understand the cultural context surrounding education equity. Kazin writes that in the war between liberals and conservatives that characterized the 1960s, the conservatives actually won most of the battles. Today's cultural landscape is littered with their mantras, now part of the national conventional wisdom: Government is too big, taxes too high, affirmative action is unfair, business is overregulated, and school choice will improve education. But conservatives did not win all the battles. Kazin believes that the decade's most successful social crusade was feminism, a movement that restructured U.S. society.

Commentators now proclaim on the airwaves that gender bias no longer exists, except for men who are victimized by feminists. Their efforts are not without success: Today the word *feminist* carries as many negative as positive connotations. So what is an educator to believe?

Those who believe in gender equity face an uphill struggle. Each time I begin a training program to help educators detect and eliminate bias from their classroom teaching, I am reminded of what some call *gender blindness* (Bailey, Scantlebury, & Letts 1997, p. 29). Often I show a videotape with subtle, if pervasive, gender bias. Asked to evaluate the tape, most teachers miss the bias. After practicing some rudimentary coding of classroom interactions, we go back to the tape. Surprise, surprise! Now the gender bias is overwhelming. No longer political or personal, the bias has become a research reality, their reality, and the teachers are motivated to create equitable teaching strategies. But why the initial gender block?

In *Failing at Fairness*, Myra Sadker and I described "a syntax of sexism so elusive that most teachers and students were completely unaware of its influence" (1995, p. 2). Teacher education and staff development programs do little to prepare teachers to see the subtle, unintentional, but damaging gender bias that still characterizes classrooms.

But subtlety is not the only reason for the persistence of inequity. A false sense of accomplishment had also taken root. We have made wonderful advances, especially in the area of access to schools, courses, and careers. Although bias is less problematic today, it still permeates and influences our classrooms.

What is the salient and current research on gender progress and problems in school? What are the disturbing cultural developments that have distorted and politicized educational equity? To answer these questions, I will borrow a device used by a late night television host: A *top 10 list*.

THE TOP 10 GENDER BIAS UPDATES

Update #10: *Segregation still thrives in U.S. schools.*

Title IX has breached the walls of the Citadel and the Virginia Military Institute, and females are now admitted to all tax-supported educational institutions. Too often, however, courses of study and careers remain gender-specific.

- The majority of females major in English, French, Spanish, music, drama, and dance, whereas males populate computer science, physics, and engineering programs.

- A recent study of 14 school-to-work programs revealed that over 90 percent of females cluster in a few traditional careers: allied health careers, teaching and education, graphic arts, and office technology (American Association of University Women Educational Foundation [hereafter AAUWEF] 1998, p. 88).

- Although almost half of medical and law students are female, they are concentrated in a few "female friendly" (and lower-paying) specialties (Sadker & Sadker 1995, p. 194).

Update #9: *Public schools are now creating single-gender classes and schools.*

More than a century ago, most schools were gender segregated. Some private schools still are. And the research on their effectiveness, at least for the girls, is compelling, if not universally accepted. In response to this research and the pressures of assertive parents (usually of girls), public school districts have openly and sometimes surreptitiously created their own single-gender classes or schools. Is this a positive or a negative development?

- If we were to implement and carefully research a limited trial of single-gender public schools and classes, the findings could improve public coed schools for boys as well as for girls. However, the current approach has the potential to fractionalize our society. In short, creating single-gender classes and schools is not a substitute for ensuring equitable public education for all our students.

Update #8: *Gender-related safety and health concerns continue to plague females.*

One hundred years ago, the argument against female education centered on health. Doctors warned that education redirected blood initially destined for the ovaries to the brain. The result: Educated women would be less likely to reproduce and more likely to go insane. The doctors' prescription: Keep girls out of school. It sounds bizarre, but it was a sign of how people viewed female health issues. Today, our attention turns to more genuine and pressing health risks.

- Twenty percent of school-age girls report being physically or sexually abused, and 80 percent report experiencing some form of sexual harassment.

- Although research shows that physical activity leads to higher self-esteem and lifelong health benefits, girls are only half as likely as boys to participate in physical education.

Update #7: *The dropout rate is not what we think it is.*

- Most educators know that boys repeat grades and drop out of school at higher rates than girls. However, few realize that girls who repeat a grade are more likely to drop out of school than male grade repeaters. When girls drop out of school, often because of pregnancy, they are less likely to return and complete school than boys. In 1995, for example, approximately one-third of Hispanic females between 16 and 24 had not completed school and had not passed a high school equivalency test.

- Boys drop out with a "crash" whereas girls drop out more quietly and more permanently.

<u>Update #6</u>: *For girls, gifted programs are often "early in and early out".*

- Elementary school gifted programs identify girls in equal or in greater numbers than boys. However, by 10th grade, girls begin to drop out of these programs at a higher rate than boys.
- Boys are more likely to take math and science gifted programs while girls are more likely to be found in gifted programs that focus on language arts. For both girls and boys, gifted programs reinforce gender segregation.

<u>Update #5</u>: *Gender bias also affects males.*

Because men earn more money, manage most organizations, and dominate both government offices and sports arenas, many Americans assume that men are the victors in the great gender divide. In fact, sexism harms men as well as women, and Title IX protects both genders. Boys are stereotyped into gender roles earlier and more rigidly than females. Three out of four boys report that they were targets of sexual harassment—usually taunts challenging their masculinity. Males who express an interest in careers typically thought of as "feminine" also encounter social pressures. The percentage of males in elementary teaching, for instance, is smaller today than when Title IX became law a quarter of a century ago.

- Although females receive lower grades on many high-stakes tests, males receive lower course grades (AAUWEF 1998, pp. 27-33). Males are less likely to have close friends and are more likely to endure alienation and loneliness throughout life. Males, after all, experience higher mortality rates through accidents, violence, and suicide. From schoolyard shootings to low humanities enrollments, boys conform to negative male stereotypes, and educators need to discourage male gender stereotyping.

Classroom interactions between teachers and students put males in the spotlight and relegate females to the sidelines.

- Studies of teacher discourse underscore male dominance in the classroom. Teachers unconsciously make males the center of instruction and give them more frequent and focused attention. Some boys do not want this attention and some girls may not notice or may prefer this lack of attention (Feldhusen & Willard-Holt 1993). The impact on both genders can be costly. Increased teacher attention contributes to enhanced student performance. Girls lose out in this equation. African American girls, for example, are assertive and outgoing when they enter school, yet they grow more passive and quiet thorough the school years (AAUWEF 1998, p.49). Boys reap the benefits of a more intense educational climate.

Update #3: *The math and science gender gap is getting smaller.*

The idea that boys outperform girls in math and science has received national attention, and that attention is paying off.

- During the 1990s female enrollment increased in many math and science courses. Honors as well as advanced placement courses showed enrollment gains.

- Girls are now more likely than boys to take biology and chemistry courses, whereas physics is still a male domain. Boys, however, are more likely to take all three core sciences–physics, chemistry, and biology (AAUWEF 1998, p. 13).

- Tests continue to reflect a gender gap, particularly high-stakes tests like the SAT. Although the gap has decreased in recent years, males continue to outscore females on both the math and verbal sections of the SAT. Boys outscore girls on math and science achievement tests, whereas females outscore males on the verbal section of the ACT. Although girls take more advanced placement exams in all courses except math, science, and computers, boys earn higher advanced placement scores and are more likely to receive college credit (AAUWEF 1998, pp. 35-41).

Update #2: *A new gender gap exists in technology.*

Certainly, the greatest change in education in recent years is the technology explosion, with the majority of US schools now connected to the Internet. But boys are more wired into this revolution than girls are.

- Boys enter school with more computer experience than girls and girls know it. Girls rate themselves significantly lower on computer ability.

- Stereotyping is alive and well in the tech world. Girls are more likely to enroll in word processing and clerical courses, whereas boys are more likely to enroll in advanced computer science and computer design classes. Both print and Internet resources continue to promote sex stereotyping, with males portrayed in powerful and prestigious technological positions (Knupfer 1998).

Update #1: *Some political forces are intent on reversing many gains in educational equity made during the past decade.*

Thirty years ago, when Myra and I first began to research gender bias, we thought that the task was pretty straightforward. First we would objectively analyze schools to see whether bias really existed. If we found bias, we would then document the inequities and work on solutions. We thought that armed with knowledge, people would want to change. Not so simple.

Educational equity is a political issue. Ultraconservatives have created "educational research" to discredit the decades of studies documenting gender bias in schools. The Women's Freedom Network is one such group that sponsors attacks not only on the research but also on the integrity and motivations of the researchers. With generous private funding and contacts with talk show hosts, news commentators, and even mainline periodicals, these "media experts" launch their attacks.

In the past, the enemies of equity spoke more openly about their beliefs: the "natural" roles of men and women, the "biological destinies" of each, even biblical references to explain the "second-class" status of females. A new day requires new tactics. The Internet and the media do not evaluate the qualifications of researchers. As a result, individuals who make up in colorful commentary what they lack in research qualifications attack the lifework of competent researchers. I regret the ultimate cost that such tactics have on the lives of children.

CULTURAL SUPPORT OF SEXISM

After practicing techniques to identify the subtle gender bias embedded in her classroom behavior, a teacher education student at the University of Wisconsin wrote:

> **I really didn't think [gender bias] was very prevalent, particularly because it can be subtle. I especially didn't think I would ever do it. But . . . I had also called on the boys more, not realizing. They were being quiet, instead of noisy, and I called on them to reward them; they could pick out the next book. Yet the girls had been good the entire time, yet I hadn't called on them at all.** (Lunderberg 1997, p. 59)

What is unusual about the story is not that the student could not see the bias; rather, it is that she was enrolled in a teacher education program that included such fundamental research training.

In a recent national study of mathematics and science methods, professors Campbell and Sanders (1997) found that two-thirds of education professors spent less than two hours teaching about gender equity and that they rarely provided practical classroom strategies to neutralize bias. More than half the professors were satisfied with this limited treatment. Why has teacher education been so slow to teach about and respond to gender bias?

One explanation may be the social resistance to feminism, female concerns, and even gender studies. In one study, students taking 17 different courses received a Sociology of Gender course syllabus developed and taught by a fictitious "Wendy Barker". The students rated the syllabus. Many students indicated that the course was imbued with bias, promoted a political agenda, and contained exams and papers that were too subjective. Although all students showed a bias against the female instructor, the bias was strongest among male students. When a similar group of students received the same syllabus, this time developed and taught by "William Barker", a fictitious male, the evaluations were more positive. Now the course was rated as less biased, the work appeared fair and reasonable, and the instructor was credible and available to students. Taught by a male, the same course seemed more comprehensive and attractive to students (Moore & Trahan 1977).

Many female administrators, teachers, professors, and counselors share similar experiences, believing that they must work harder simply to be considered equal. Males have an unspoken, often unconscious sense of entitlement, which is reflected in their belief that they influence school policy. Female teachers do not express similar feelings of power and influence (Lee, Loeb, & Marks 1995). No wonder, then, that political forces can exploit female alienation and cultural resistance to feminism to promote their social agenda.

What are educators to do? Individual educators, teachers, and administrators need to ensure that instructional strategies and curricular innovations benefit all our children. Twenty-five years after Title IX, we must celebrate our progress and recommit ourselves to finishing the job.

ABOUT THE AUTHOR

David Sadker is a Professor of Education at American University, Washington, DC. Together with his late wife, Myra, he co-authored numerous books and articles, including Failing at Fairness. Their 1982 Sex Equity Handbook for Schools has been an eye-opener for every educator. He is currently completing the sixth edition of Teachers, Schools, and Society (McGraw-Hill), an introduction to education. He is the recipient of many grants and awards for his work on sex equity in education.

REFERENCES

AAUWEF - (American Association of University Women Educational Foundation [1998]). *Gender gaps: Where our schools fail our children.* Washington, DC: Author.

Bailey, B.L, Scantlebury, K., & Letts, W. J. (1997, January/February). It's not my style: Using disclaimers to ignore issues in science. *Journal of Teacher Education*, (48)1, 29-35.

Campbell, P. B., & Sanders, J. (1997, January/February). Uniformed but interested: Findings of a national survey on gender equity in preservice teacher education. *Journal of Teacher Education*, 48(1), 69-75.

Feldhusen, F, F., & Willard-Holt, C. (1993). Gender differences in classroom Interactions and career aspirations of gifted students. *Contemporary Educational Psychology*, 18, 355-362.

Kazin, M. (in press). *Like a Civil War. The United States in the 1960s.* Oxford, England: Oxford University Press.

Knupfer, N.N. (1998, Winter). Gender divisions across technology advertisement and the www: Implications for educational equity. *Theory into Practice, 37(1)*, 54-63.

Lee, V. E., Loeb, S., & Marks, H. M. (1995, May). Gender differences in secondary school teachers control over classroom and school policy. *American Journal of Education*, 103, 259-301.

Lunderberg, M. A. (1997, January/February). You guys are overreacting: Teaching Prospective teachers about subtle gender bias. *Journal of Teacher Education*, 48(1), 55-61.

Moore, M., & Trahan, R. (1997, December). Biased and political: Student perceptions of females teaching about gender. *College Student Journal*, 31, 434-444.

Sadker, M., & Sadker, D. (1995). *Failing at fairness: How our schools cheat girls.* New York: Touchstone Press.

A CASE FOR STUDYING SEXISM
IN THE ESL CLASSROOM
by
Mary Yepez
Bergen Community College, NJ

ABSTRACT

This paper presents a case for conducting research on gender issues and their impact in American classrooms of English as a Second Language (ESL). Research has been (and is still being) conducted on how gender influences teacher responses in non-ESL classrooms, and pedagogical issues have been delved into at length in the study of ESL classrooms. However, the study of gender in ESL classrooms is still at an early stage. Synopses of recent and ongoing studies of gender in the ESL classroom and in American non-ESL classrooms are presented and discussed, and topics that could further the research are outlined.

INTRODUCTION: *Studying Sexism in the ESL Classroom*

The American classroom has been shown to be dramatically conducive to gender-inequitable treatment. Research conducted in American classrooms over the last 30 years shows that a preference for males exists at all levels of educational environments, from elementary schools to graduate institutions (Sadker & Sadker 1992, 1999, Hall 1982, Spaulding 1963, Brophy & Good 1974, 1990). Most teachers are unaware that they have gender-based preconceptions about students (Rosenthal & Jacobsen 1968). The preconceptions have been shown to influence teacher behavior and the performance expectations teachers have of students (Brophy & Good 1974), as well as to affect negatively a student's actual classroom performance. Teachers are also unaware of the extent these notions influence their own behavior (Sadker *et al.* 1999). Non-ESL teachers have, at best, minimal awareness of gender. In fact, at the university level, faculty members are generally inclined to want to treat their female students fairly (Hall 1982). However, they are frequently unaware of biases in their behavior, which may mean that differential treatment of the sexes could be unintentional (Sadker *et al.* 1999). Teachers frequently maintain the gender inequities that already exist in society (Wilkinson & Marrett 1985).

As English as a Second Language (ESL) classes are usually at the college level, the demonstrated teacher preference for males means that females in American ESL classrooms could conceivably have a less than optimal experience learning the English language (as teacher attitudes are a major factor in establishing and shaping a classroom dynamic). Other societal factors can place female students in ESL classrooms at risk for having a negative pedagogical experience in American ESL classrooms. In American universities, females have been shown to receive less informal feedback, encouragement, and praise than males for their efforts (Sadker & Sadker 1982, 1989, 1992). These subtle and overt inequities yielded feelings of discouragement, anger, or confusion by female graduate students (Hall 1982). They eventually resulted in the females experiencing feelings of being silenced, making it less likely that they would continue their studies to more advanced levels (Women's Student Coalition 1980).

Unconscious teacher expectations and societal structures traditional in teachers' and students' cultures too, can lead to potentially unequal treatment of male and female students (Yepez 1999). More aggressive males might attract more of a teacher's attention in an ESL class, leading to less teacher-to-female interaction. There is no reason to assume teacher sensitivity would not extend to gender issues, but the pro-male bias detailed in the literature on gender inequity in the classroom warrants a closer look at teacher interaction patterns with male and female students specifically in the ESL classroom. Therefore, it is imperative that teacher trainers and ESL program planners study the presence and effects of sexism on the pedagogical process in the American ESL classroom.

PAST STUDIES ON GENDER AND ESL

Some aspects of language acquisition, such as turn-taking, and cultural differences as they affect interaction patterns of ESL teachers and their students, have been formally observed and quantified. However, research is still scant on gender's specific role as a variable in teacher-student interaction patterns in the ESL classroom. Little ESL literature has been published that might alert an ESL teacher to possible gender biases in his or her pedagogic interactions with male and female students. Research methods on gender and interactions in a classroom have typically involved observation with pre-set coding schemes that focus on few dimensions of talk, and on questionnaires that tap attitudes and perceptions (Thorne, Kramarae & Henley 1983).

Two researchers who have focused their attention on gender in the ESL classroom are Mary Yepez and Rebecca L. Oxford. In a study of four American ESL teachers, Yepez (1991) sought to determine how ESL teachers *perceive* their treatment of the genders versus their actual distribution of interaction frequency and attention among the genders. She also examined whether certain factors in each teacher's background might have led to the discovered interactional behavior patterns with the teacher's male and female students. Yepez (1991) quantified her observations using the Interactions for Sex Equity in Classroom Teaching (INTERSECT) instrument. INTERSECT, which was developed in 1982 by Myra and David Sadker, seminal researchers on gender in education at American University in Washington D.C., was selected for its ability to facilitate analysis of gender interaction patterns and equity or inequity in a multi-ethnic classroom in the U.S. The four American ESL teachers observed by Yepez felt that some ESL teachers might engage in gender inequity in their classes. One teacher showed inequitable behavior, which supports the literature findings on gender equity in the classroom (i.e. favoring males), but that teacher attributed his behavior to an aggressive Latin American male student who dominated the class as a whole.

Oxford's research (1993, 2000) on learning styles and strategies in the American ESL classroom focused on the differences found between the genders. Styles are the preferred means of absorbing and integrating information, and strategies are the cognitive tools and behaviors developed as a result of discovered styles. Each learning style uses different strategies to absorb and integrate the knowledge of a second language. Strategies help learners to enhance their understanding, storage, retrieval, and ultimate use of information (Rigney 1978). Both learning styles and strategies are frequently linked to gender (Ehrman & Oxford 1988, Oxford & Ehrman 1988, Oxford 1990, 1993, Nyikos 1990), and the development of learning styles and strategies frequently differs on gender lines (Nyikos, 1990). For example, Gass and Varonis (1986), in their study of the conversational behavior of second language learners, found that men will dominate conversations, while women will initiate more "negotiations of meaning", trying to understand and communicate clearly. Oxford (1993) believes these behavior patterns reflect the general tendencies of men and women in native language use. Oxford also found that if learners are not pressed by the teacher or the classroom dynamics, they will apply second language learning strategies that fit closely with their favorite learning style. The style that will dominate will frequently depend on the favored learning styles and strategies of the teacher, regardless of gender (1993). Awareness and further study of gender and ESL are imperative if all students, male and female, are to have optimal experiences in the ESL classroom.

GENDER DIFFERENCES AND CLASSROOM INEQUITIES

Thoughtless inequities in the classroom can stem from textbooks, instructional materials, and teacher attitudes (Sadker & Sadker 1982), and can hamper female learning of a second language. As gender-differentiated treatment starts before students reach the classroom, and teachers then perpetuate the patterns (Brophy & Good 1990), response behavior in early years may set future behavior with teachers, perhaps causing teachers to react differently to the sexes (Huston & Carpenter 1985).

In the early years of schooling, American females outperform males, but American males eventually gain more prominence and ultimately outperform females. By junior high school, males call out more than females, and teachers are more likely to accept called-out answers from males, whereas females who call out are ignored (Morse & Eman 1969). Males also receive more time, instruction, praise, extended conversation, criticism, and direction on how to do things for themselves (Wilkinson & Marrett 1985). Teachers initiate more contacts with male students (Jones 1971), and male students are asked more open-ended and abstract questions than are females (Sikes 1971), who are either left alone or teachers do their tasks for them.

Males also demand more teacher attention than females (Maccoby & Jacklin 1974), and they receive it. In their research on interaction distribution, Eccles & Blumenfeld (1985) found that males not only receive more teacher talk than females, but also more than the group as a whole. Males had 39% of all communication directed at them, and females only 29%. The group as a whole had the remaining 32%. Males also receive comparatively more praise for academic ability and less criticism for intellectual inadequacy than do females (Dweck et al. 1978). In their study of praise and criticism patterns, Dweck and her colleagues found that 90% of male-directed praise was for academic ability, compared to 80% for the females. The remainder of the praise was for following rules. Of criticism directed to females 90% was for intellectual inadequacy, compared with 50% of male-directed criticism (with the remainder for not following rules). Clearly, expectations can lead to differential treatment of male and female students (Wilkinson & Marrett 1985). Educators may not always be aware of the impact that differences (including gender differences) between students might have on a student-teacher dynamic (Brophy & Good 1974). But as teacher self-awareness of these behaviors is low, it would stand to reason that if males get more attention, then females are ignored more (Yepez 1999).

Teacher self-awareness in interactions with male and female students can make teachers more sensitive to their behavior toward the genders (Sadker & Sadker 1999). Teachers must therefore become more aware of their behavior so that they can exert more control over their teaching and improve the classroom atmosphere for females.

THE ROLE OF CULTURE

The cultures of both teachers and students in an American classroom strongly influence student learning (Brophy & Good 1990), and should be taken into account in any study of sexism in an American ESL classroom. Though most ESL teachers in the US have special training in cultural sensitivity, the training frequently does not address possible gender bias and how it can be expressed in a classroom. ESL teachers in the US, for example, might expect females to dominate an ESL classroom in much the same way American females dominate foreign language classrooms; they might pay more attention to their female students. However, individuals of diverse nationalities, cultures, and races enroll in American ESL classes, and each has his or her own socially and culturally inculcated behavior patterns and ideas about males and females. These patterns, especially if the students are from cultures that systematically silence women, could shape American ESL classroom behavior patterns, and ESL teachers lacking cultural sensitivity and awareness might allow their classrooms to become male-dominated. Foreign females in ESL classrooms would then receive even less teacher attention and interaction time.

In non-English speaking countries, language learning is considered a male activity. Foreign males are considered better language-learners than their American counterparts (Brophy & Good 1974). A worry is that male students from countries in Africa and Western Europe, for example, where males dominate language learning, could drown out females in American ESL classrooms the way American males drown out females in math and science classes (Yepez 1994). This would hamper female efforts to acquire English as a second language in the US, since interaction is crucial in the ESL classroom and language learning is an interactive skill.

THE COLLEGE CLASSROOM

As many ESL classes in the US are conducted at the college level, data from observations of American college classrooms must be taken into account in any study of sexism in the US ESL classroom. Natural segregating patterns among humans can play a role in teacher interaction patterns, as they apply to race as well as gender. Genders tend to segregate naturally in American society, with males and females grouping separately in classroom settings (Maccoby & Jacklin 1974).

The Sadkers (1982) described a teacher behavior they call "mind sex" where teachers call on students of the same sex one after the other. Even though teachers exhibited this behavior with both sexes, they called more persistently on males.

Measuring organizational characteristics, such as seating in a classroom and indeed in a school, can illuminate teacher-student and student-student interaction dynamics (Eder & Hallinan 1978). Yepez (1991) found that students tend to congregate together by sex and that the sex of the teacher determined which sex of the students congregated closer to the front of the classroom.

Up until college, Sadker & Sadker (1985) found that the overall number of interactions for both males and females decreased throughout the course of schooling, and the proportion of "silent" students increased at later years of schooling. In the fourth, sixth, and eighth-grade classes studied, 25% of the students did not interact with the teacher at all. In college classes, the share of non-interactors rose to 50% (Sadker & Sadker 1985). College women in particular become increasingly silent as they progressed through college. They also experience a decline in self-esteem (Hall 1982) because of comparative teacher inattention and because females receive more criticism for lack of knowledge and skill (Dweck et al. 1978).

How faculty members interact with their students has also been shown to be of great importance in a classroom dynamic. Female professors are involved in more classroom give-and-take than male professors, who are harsher and frequently reprimand students publicly (Richardson, Cook, & Macke 1981). Students in female teachers' classes initiate more interactions with the teachers, (Kajander 1976). However, both male-taught and female-taught classes show the same amount of interaction with the sexes—both favor males (Wilkinson & Marrett 1985).

Among the issues concerning sexism in university-level classes cited by Hall (1982) in her report on classroom climate and how it affects women at the university level are that some faculty members, inadvertently or purposefully, interact differently with male and female students in ways that discourage female participation. For example, teachers may call on males more often than females (Hall 1982). They may also make more eye contact with males than with females (Thorne 1979), thereby inviting more male response. They may also ask men higher-order questions that demand critical thought (Sadker & Sadker 1982), allow men to interrupt women in class discussions (Hall 1982), and encourage men to think for themselves far more than they do women. Women may also receive less informal feedback, encouragement, and praise than men for their academic efforts (Dweck *et al.* 1978). The issue of awareness is of particular interest considering interruptions. Some professors are unaware that they interrupt females more often than males, or that they allow women to be easily interrupted in class discussions (Thorne *et al.* 1983), which can lead women to believe that their views are not being listened to and/or taken as seriously as those of their male peers (Hall 1982).

Nonverbal behavior can also shape the classroom climate. Teacher signals can indicate inclusion and exclusion, show interest and attention, communicate expectations of students' success or failure, and foster or impede students' confidence in their own abilities (Yepez 1999). Teachers, for example, may encourage males by making more eye contact, nodding and gesturing more often in response to male questions, leaning forward when men speak, and selecting men as student assistants (Henley 1977). On the other hand, they may discourage females by looking at the clock when women speak, or by making direct sexual overtures to their female students (Hall 1982). Faculty members also discourage females in the classroom by ignoring women students while recognizing men (even when women have clearly volunteered for a task), calling directly on men and not women, waiting longer for men than women to answer a question before going on to another student, and using the generic "he" or "man" to represent both men and women.

Female minority students are subject to a range of disparaging classroom behaviors by faculty members in college and graduate school classrooms. Among the behaviors most frequently reported are ignoring, interrupting (Noonan 1980), maintaining physical distance, avoiding eye contact, offering little guidance and criticism (Noonan 1980, Duncan 1976), and attributing female success to luck or factors other than ability (Noonan 1980). These could conceivably spill over to American ESL classrooms, with the many ethnicities that are frequently represented in them.

Still, whether conscious or unconscious, differential treatment based on sex is far from harmless. Consistent denigration of female intellectual expression can damage not only individual students, but also the educational process itself (Yepez 1999). If overt disparaging remarks or more subtle differential behaviors occur frequently, especially when the perpetrators of these remarks or behaviors are gatekeepers who teach required courses, act as advisors, or serve as chairs of departments, females are at a distinct disadvantage. Such behaviors can have a profoundly negative impact on women's academic and career development by discouraging female classroom participation, by preventing women from seeking help outside of class, causing them to avoid or drop certain classes, switch majors or subspecialties within majors, and in some instances, even leave a given institution. All these behaviors minimize development of the individual collegial relationships with faculty, which are crucial for a student's future professional development, and dampen career aspirations as well as undermine confidence (El-Khawas 1980).

SELF-ESTEEM

Self-esteem is an important factor in successful second language acquisition, particularly in light of cross-cultural aspects of second language learning (Brodkey & Shore 1976, Gardner & Lambert 1972). A systematically experienced pro-male bias in a classroom can undermine a female student's self-esteem, thereby limiting her ability to acquire English in an American ESL classroom. According to Brown (1980), student self-esteem is one of the main factors of human behavior that contributes to learning a second language. A study Brown cited of research conducted by Adelaide Heyde in 1979 on the acquisition of French as a second language among American college students found that students with high levels of self-esteem performed better in French as a foreign language. Heyde also found that the highest correlation occurred between high self-esteem and oral performance.

Educators studying gender in the classroom have found that gender-inequitable behavior causes low self-esteem in females, which interferes with their general education (Sears & Feldman 1966, Ehrman & Oxford 1988). The correlation between high self-esteem and optimal second language acquisition indicates that gender inequity in a classroom could lead to lower self-esteem in females, which would impede female acquisition of a second language.

TOPICS FOR FURTHER INVESTIGATION

The ESL classroom must be studied to determine if gender inequities exist, and the educational community must be made aware of the dynamics of gender in the ESL classroom. Among the everyday inequities carried into the classroom worth quantifying in a study of sexism are: men talk more than women; men talk longer and take more turns at speaking; men control topics more often than do women; men interrupt women more frequently than women interrupt men; men's interruptions of women more often introduce trivial personal comments that bring the women's discussion to an end or change the focus of the topic (Thorne *et al.*, 1983).

The elements that need to be studied are: frequency and nature of teacher interactions with gender. Variables such as race and culture, teacher backgrounds, and eventual student performance in the class, correlate to determine whether sexist attitudes do indeed negatively impact on female performance. In addition, when designing studies, researchers should pay close attention to the age, demographic, and cultural characteristics of their sample as well as to the type of materials and content being covered (Brophy & Good 1990).

Roberta Hall (1982) cited several areas for further research on sexism in the classroom, which would be strongly applicable for research in the ESL classroom. They include:

- The relationship of the sex ratio of a given class to patterns of interaction.

- The factors (aside from proportion of men and women students) that make some classes highly sex-differentiated and others less so.

- The differentiation of verbal and nonverbal patterns by race and by age both within and between the sexes.

- The similarities between subtle differential treatment of students based on sex and based on race.

- The relationship between sex of a teacher and sex of a student as it may affect both classroom behavior and education and professional outcomes.

- The effect of interactions between men and women faculty on men and women students.

- The identification of those areas which women students may most benefit from, and special efforts in creating a learning climate to counter the effects of prior experiences in school and society.

Teacher training can help teachers to become more equitable and effective, which could reduce and even eliminate sex bias from classroom interactions. It would be irresponsible to be complacent about the gender equity issue; it deserves rigorous attention as a sociolinguistic variable. In addition, the development of awareness about the pitfalls of possible sex bias in the ESL classroom should be a part of the ESL teacher's training so that ESL professionals can be sensitive to their own pedagogy and self-understanding. A far greater number of qualitative strategies are needed if we are to hope to understand the thoughts, impulses, and beliefs that lie behind the gender interactions found in American ESL classrooms.

NB: *This paper was first published in "Working papers on language, gender and sexism". Vol. 4, # 2 in 1994.*

ABOUT THE AUTHOR

Mary Yepez is Assistant Professor of English at Bergen Community College in N.J. She is a recipient of a Fulbright Fellowship, Harvard Administration Fellowship, New York University Doctoral Fellowship, and Roothbert Fund Fellowship. She has taught in Japan, the Czech Republic, and Spain, as well as in the US.

REFERENCES

Brodkey, David & Helen Shore (1976). Student personality and success in an English language program. *Language Learning* 26: 153-159.

Brophy, Jere & Thomas H. Good (1974). *Teacher student relationships: Causes and consequences.* New York: Holt, Rinehart, and Winston.

Brophy, Jere & Thomas H. Good (1990). *Educational psychology: A realistic approach (4E).* Reading, MA: Addison-Wesley.

Brown, Douglas (1980). *Principles of language learning and teaching.* Englewood Cliffs, NJ: Prentice Hall.

Duncan, B. (1976). Minority Students. In J. Katz and R.T. Harnett (eds.) *Scholars in the making: The Development of Graduate and Professional Students.* Cambridge, MA.

Dweck, Carol, William Davidson, Sharon Nelson & Bradley Enna (1979). Sex Differences in learned helplessness: II, The contingencies of evaluation feedback in the classroom, and III, an experimental analysis. *Developmental Psychology 14: 198-210.*

Eccles, Jaquelynne S., & Phyllis Blumenfeld (1985). Classroom experiences and student gender: Are there differences, and do they matter? In L.C. Wilkinson and C.B. Marrett (eds.), *Gender influences in classroom interaction.* Orlando FL: Academic Press.

Eder, Diane, & Mary T. Hallinan (1978). Sex differences in children's friendships. *American Sociological Review 41: 237-250.*

Ehrman, M.E. & Rebecca L. Oxford (1988). Ants & grasshoppers, badgers & butterflies: Qualitative and quantitative exploration of adult language learning styles strategies. Columbus, OH. Paper presented at the Symposium on Research Perspectives for Adult Language Learning and Acquisition, Ohio State University.

El-Khawas, Elaine (1980). Differences in academic development during college. In *Men and women learning together: A study of college students in late '70s.* Providence, RI: Office of the Provost, Brown University.

Gardner, Robert & Wallace E. Lambert (1972). *Attitudes and motivation in second language learning.* Rowley, MA: Newbury House.

Gass, Susan H. and Evangeline M. Varonis (1986). Sex differences in NNS/NNS Interactions. In R. Day (ed.) *Talking to learn: Conversation in second language acquisition.* Rowley, MA: Newbury House.

Grant, Linda (1983). The socialization of white females in classrooms. Montreal, Canada. Paper presented at the annual meeting of the American Educational Research Association, April.

Hall, Roberta (1982). *The classroom climate. A chilly one for women?* Washington D.C: Association of American Colleges, Project on the Status of Women.

Henley, Nancy (1977). *The Body Politics: Power, sex and nonverbal communication.* Englewood Cliffs, NJ: Prentice-Hall, Inc.

Huston, Aletha C. & Jan Carpenter (1985). Gender differences in preschool classrooms: The effects of sex-typed activity choices. In L.C. Wilkinson and C.B. Marrett (eds.) *Gender influences in classroom interaction.* Orlando FL: Academic Press.

Jones, Vernon Frank (1971). The influence of teacher-student introversion, achievement and similarity on teacher-student dyadic classroom interaction. Austin, TX. Unpublished doctoral dissertation, University of Texas Austin.

Kajander, Carol (1976). The effects of instructor and student sex on verbal behavior in college classrooms. *Dissertation Abstracts International* 37 (5-A): 2743-2744.

Maccoby, Eleanor, & Carol Jacklin (1974). *The psychology of sex differences.* Stanford, CA: Stanford University Press.

Morse, Benjamin W. & Virginia A. Eman (1969). The construct of androgyny: An Overview and implications of research. In C.L. Berryman and V.A. Eman (eds). *Proceedings of the First Annual Conference on Communication, Language and Sex.* Rowley, MA: Newbury House, 76-90.

Noonan, John F. (1980). White faculty and black students: Examining assumptions and Practices. Unpublished paper, The center for Improving teacher effectiveness. Richmond, VA: Virginia Commonwealth University.

Nyikos, M. (1990). Sex-related differences in adult language learning: Socialization and memory factors. *Modern Language Journal* 74(3): 273-287.

Oxford, Rebecca L. (1990). La difference continue... gender differences in Second/foreign language learning styles and strategies. In J. Sunderland (ed.) *Exploring Gender.* Englewood Cliffs, NJ: Prentice-Hall.

Oxford, Rebecca L. (1993). Evidence and instructional implications of gender differences in second/foreign language (L2) learning styles and strategies. Unpublished paper.

Oxford, Rebecca L. & Ehrman, M. (1988). Psychological type and adult language learning strategies: A pilot study. *Journal of Psychological Type* 16: 22-32.

Richardson, Lloyd, Jean Cook & Anne Macke (1981). Classroom management and strategies of male and female university professors In Lloyd Richardson and Vera Taylor (eds.) *Issues in sex, gender and society.* Lexington, MA: Heath.

Rigney, J. W. (1978). Learning strategies: A theoretical perspective. In H.F. O'Neil (ed). *Learning strategies.* New York: Academic Press.

Rosenthal, Robert & Leonore Jacobsen (1968). *Pygmalion in the classroom: Teacher expectation and pupil?s intellectual development.* New York: Holt, Rinehart and H. Winston.

Sadker, Myra & David Sadker (1982). *Sex equity handbook for schools.* New York: Longman Press.

— (1985). Sexism in schools of the 80s. *Psychology Today* March: 25-28.

— (1987). Sex, sexism and the preparation of educators. *Peabody Journal of education* 64 (4): 213-4.

— (1989). Gender equity and educational reform. *Educational Leadership* 46 (6): 44-7.

— (1992). Ensuring equitable participation in college classes. *New Directions for Teaching and Learning 49 Teaching for diversity:* 49-56.

— (1999). Gender Equity: Still knocking at the classroom door. Educational Leadership. April: 22-26.

Sears, Pauline, & David Feldman (1966). Teacher interactions with boys and girls. *National Elementary Principal* 46: 30-5.

Sikes, Joseph Nevill (1971). Differential behavior of male and female teachers with male and female students. Austin, TX: Unpublished doctoral dissertation, University of Texas at Austin.

Spaulding, Robert (1963). *Achievement, creativity, and self-concept correlates of teacher-pupil transactions in elementary school.* Washington, D.C: Dept. of Health, Education, and Welfare.

Thorne, Barrie (1979). Claiming verbal space: Women, speech & language for college classroom. Paper presented at the Research Conference on Educational Environments and the Undergraduate Woman. Wellesly, M.A.

Thorne, Barrie, Cheris Kramarae & Nancy Henley (1983). *Language, gender, and society*. Rowley, MA: Newbury House.

Wilkinson, Louise Cheryl, & Cora Marrett (eds. 1985). Gender influences in classroom interaction. Orlando: Academic Press.

Women's Student Coalition (1980, June). *The quality of women's education at Harvard University: A survey of sex discrimination in the graduate and professional schools.* Cambridge, MA: Harvard University.

Yepez, Mary (1991). An analysis of four ESL teachers' interaction patterns with adult male and female ESL students. New York: Unpublished doctoral dissertation, New York University.

Yepez, Mary (1994). An Observation of gender specific sexism in the ESL classroom. *Sex Roles.* vol. 30 #1 and #2 (Jan).

Yepez, Mary (1994). A Case for Studying Sexism in the ESL Classroom. *Working papers on language, gender and sexism.* Vol. 4.2 (Dec).

Yepez, Mary (1994). Are ESL male and female students being treated fairly? Some Solutions. M.Aldridge (ed.). Diversity in Oneness. Kendall Publications: NY.

Yepez Mary, (1999). Sexism in the ESL classroom-Pedagogical implications. *Ram's Horn:* Dartmouth College: NH.

Using Inclusive Language in the ESOL Classroom:
THE MEDUSA SYNDROME
by
Effie Papatzikou Cochran
John Jay College of Criminal Justice - CUNY

ABSTRACT

After briefly indicating the long record of linguistic sex discrimi-nation and the stratagems it has forced women to devise, this paper asserts that the 19th and 20th century feminist movement has brought modern western societies -- and their languages -- to a period of transition. This uncertain, transitional time finds insecure men caught in a "Medusa syndrome", threatened and uneasy about their personal and professional futures in an era of feminist advancement. The author is especially concerned about this phenomenon's manifestation in colleges, and particularly in the ESOL classroom. She finds female ESOL students supremely vulnerable in this context, as a result both of men's "acting out" and of women's "masochism". In an attempt to help ESL teachers address the problem, the article makes four practical recommendations: 1) open-ended classroom drama situations designed to be completed in various ways by students, 2) sensitivity to students' (particularly women students') non-verbal communication, 3) avoidance of sexist and racist language (often unintentional, but no less real), and 4) a brief but representative set of readings and reference texts on sexism and language (provided in the form of a select reading & usage list).

AN ANCIENT STRATEGY

It is not news that women have been discriminated against, even in being "placed on a pedestal", by patriarchal norms that have pertained in most societies for hundreds and even thousands of years. It is no less a fact, though one that has only recently become common knowledge, that sexual discrimina-tion in human society manifests itself in the linguistic patterns of human speech. Some cultures, for example, have developed double feminine dialects, one for women addressing women and children and another for women addressing men. Even two distinct versions of the same language are not unknown: a public male language used exclusively by men, both in public and in private, and a private female language restricted to women (Trudgill 1983). The millenia-long effect that patriarchal supremacy has had on the languages of human culture is charmingly illustrated by the following bit of dialogue from Aristophanes's Ecclesiazousae (393 B.C.) between Praxagora and one of her women co-conspirators, who are planning to infiltrate in disguise the all-male Athenian Senate for the purpose of passing community property legislation:

PRAXAGORA: ... the time's running short. Try to speak worthily, let your language be truly manly, and lean on your staff with dignity.

FIRST WOMAN: I had rather have seen one of your regular orators giving you wise advice; but, as that is not to be, it behooves me to break silence; I cannot, for my part indeed, allow the tavern-keepers to fill up their wine-pits with water. No, by the two goddesses [Demeter and Persephone] ...

PRAXAGORA: What? By the two goddesses! Wretched woman, where are your senses?

FIRST WOMAN: Eh! What? ... I have not asked you for a drink.

PRAXAGORA: No, but you want to pass for a man, and you swear by the two goddesses. Otherwise you did it very well.

FIRST WOMAN: Well then. By Apollo ...

PRAXAGORA: Stop! All these details of language must be adjusted; else it is quite useless to go to the Assembly.

(Oates & O'Neill, see also Gregersen p. 4)

Patriarchalism in social structure and androcentrism in language have long been contented bedfellows, as this little piece from one of Aristophanes's lesser comedies makes clear. But the passage also illustrates the lengths of subterfuge and deception to which women in male-dominated societies have been forced in order to exercise any sort of public influence. Most women, of course, simply accepted patriarchal conditions with the fatalism thrust upon their sex, while men ~ even men of good will ~ continued uncritically to enjoy their positions of professional, social, and familial privilege. Many, indeed, enjoyed their privilege quite consciously, believing their superior position to be justified by creation and/or philosophy: "Male comes first because it is the worthier gender" was a representative opinion among 16th and 17th century English grammarians, an opinion that sprouted from these gentlemen's Latin roots.[1] The few women who dared to dissent from such sentiments did so surreptitiously if at all.

THE OBJECTS RESPOND

In the mid-19th century, beginning with the careers of early feminists/abolitionists like Elizabeth Cady Stanton and Sojourner Truth in America, and followed a bit later by Harriet Taylor in England, along with Susan B. Anthony and Carrie Chapman Catt internationally, women at last began overtly and directly to voice their opposition to male privilege. At first, male reaction was sometimes physical and brutal (Abzug & Kelber 1984), but the need to overturn sexual inequity had been suppressed far too long; real change had become inevitable. The early feminists laid the foundations of the struggle for women's suffrage in the late 19th and early 20th centuries, out of which the women's movement of the present day has matured. Western societies now appear to be experiencing a transitional period - post-patriarchal, yet hardly matriarchal, and with the exact dimensions of the future resolution still too far off and hazy to be clearly perceived. Accordingly, men's response to those they used to term their "distaff side" has itself evolved into a new phase: For the most part, physical and vocal opposition from men towards self-determination for women has disappeared from public view. But in private there is real residual anger over lost dominance; physical abuse at home and sexual harassment in the workplace are still frighteningly common, and males now accuse women of "male bashing".

THE CONDITION DEFINED

In 1985, I coined the term "Medusa syndrome" to describe the buried anger that seems to characterize many men's response to what I have suggested is an uncertain transitional period in relationships between the sexes. The condition is a paralyzing, sometimes almost petrifying gynaekophobia experienced by insecure males, and by males inconsolable over the loss of patriarchy, when confronted by strong or dominant women, that is to say, by women in powerful or status quo threatening situations. Such men are frightened of relinquishing any more of their power to women. They are threatened by women's open insistence on equal educational and professional opportunity, and they are uneasy about women's demand for equal pay at work and ~ above all ~ for an equitable division of labor at home, especially since they can think of no cogent, rational rejoinder to such demands. Many such men "act out" their feelings, lashing out against their female subordinates, colleagues, and lovers.

AND TRACKED INTO THE COLLEGE CLASSROOM

We should not be surprised, therefore, when we discover that this kind of male-to-female behavior manifests itself among male teachers and students in the college classroom: Women's comments are taken lightly or completely ignored; in class discussions, women are constantly interrupted and on occasion blatantly put down; the woman student is treated condescendingly when she comes up with the "wrong" answer, and with surprise when "occasionally" she is right. Overall, women are treated as an exotic species in the halls of academia, especially when they dare to study in traditionally masculine fields.[2]

The syndrome described is perhaps more evident in ESOL classrooms than in "regular" academic classes, despite ESOL teachers' vaunted sensitivity to their students' emotional dynamics. In fact, the ESOL woman student has even more going against her than the average woman college student: She is often a mature adult attempting to pull herself up socially and economically by acquiring an education. She is hindered, however, in not possessing the English language facility that would permit her to accomplish her goals. Typically, she comes from the Near or Far East, Central or South America, the Caribbean, India, Africa, or an Eastern European country. Thus, she and virtually all of her sisters come from native environments that are thoroughly patriarchal. She comes into a more subtly patriarchal classroom environment, one that is perpetuated to some degree by school personnel, but that is primarily the creation of her male classmates, with whom she often shares a common culture, and who are particularly anxious to hold onto their superior male status in the light of their loss of the other privileges of which they have been stripped by becoming immigrants/refugees.

THE CAUSES HONESTLY ASSESSED

Yet we make a grievous error if we attempt to make third world male students the whole cause of the sexism suffered by women in the ESOL classroom. As has been well known since the late sixties, most societies, including so-called "progressive" western cultures, have viewed women as a class in one of two basic ways: They have either been perceived and talked about as sex objects, or their identities have been defined primarily in relationship to males. In fact, the icon of woman as appendage to man is even indicated grammatically in some languages, and as such ~ according to the Whorfian hypothesis that language influences belief ~ may be a partial cause of the cultural practices that manifest female-to-male dependence. For example, in Greek the genitive of possession in a woman's surname indicates that she "belongs" to her father-lord (before marriage) or to her husband-lord (from marriage through her husband's death and until her own). A Greek man, by contrast, is his own "lord" from birth, as evidenced by the nominative case of his surname. A similar grammatical pattern is characteristic of Russian and other languages.

The feminine stereotype has thus almost always dominated social reality: The woman's role has normally been the humble and supportive helpmate or dependent, and only rarely the proud, independent initiator. Her very identity has been defined as the son's mother, the doctor's secretary or nurse, the senator's wife, and the priest's assisting nun or daughter (Eakins & Eakins 1978). Women have experienced since childhood the feelings of rejection that are the inevitable consequence of such stereotyping. They have known what it is to be a source of disappointment to parents who wanted male offspring to carry on the father's surname. In childhood and adolescence, they have had to accept the imposition of stricter and more numerous restraints than their brothers.

Twenty-five years ago, in her article "The Making of a Non-sexist Dictionary" (Thorne & Henley 1975, pp. 57-63), Alma Graham reported some astonishing findings from her study of dictionaries and textbooks: In a society (the USA) where there were a hundred women for every ninety-five men, males -- she claimed -- occupied center stage in textbooks of all subjects, including home economics! In addition, every mother's first-born was male in the texts, and females were consistently excluded from certain activities on grounds of weakness and passivity. By the mid-eighties, the situation had improved only marginally if at all, with many college texts continuing to stereotype male and female roles and to exclude women from narrative and content (Sadker 1983). And the struggle for inclusive language and the elimination of sexual stereotyping in textbooks continues into the new millennium.

It should hardly be surprising, therefore, to find women displaying a kind of masochistic mind-set, stemming from repressed anger over a deep and usually unconscious sense of deprivation and discrimination, both in the classroom and in other contexts. In short, a set of prescribed and proscribed expectations, based on sex at birth (a biological reality), have dictated women's gender roles later in life (a social construct, and -- in languages other than English -- an arbitrary grammatical category). This condition is, of course, suffered equally by women outside the ESOL classroom, but for the female ESOL student, it compounds the difficulties to which she is already heir by virtue of her special cultural and linguistic situation.

FOUR SOLUTIONS PROPOSED

It is time for all teachers of English as an additional or foreign language to direct their own and others' attention to the predicament of the gifted but forgotten foreign-born woman in their ESOL and mainstream classrooms. The language minority female college student urgently deserves to be acknowledged, not only because of the inequity of her condition, but also because her only forum of self-expression may well be that very classroom where she begs, usually non-verbally and barely consciously, to be heard and understood. I would offer four concrete suggestions to open ourselves to the nuances of this student's problem and to enable teachers to handle her situation more expertly:

1) First, we can see to it that our classes provide explicit opportunities for students to vent and discuss their feelings through carefully planned exercises. I have found that the use of open-ended dramatic scenarios helps students to vocalize problems of discrimination. Such scenarios have the added virtue of providing opportunities for students to display their creativity and flair for the dramatic. The side effects of this sort of classroom activity are numerous. Not only is the student's self-image significantly improved, but also a variety of specific linguistic skills are strengthened in the process: Students are asked to read and comprehend an open-ended dialogue, for which they are then required to provide their own written ending before they even begin to speak the dialogue's lines; "in performance", some listen to the finished dialogue while others speak its lines clearly and correctly, and each group of students enacts the dialogue's ending according to the written version they have composed.

2) Second, ESOL teachers (perhaps more than any other teachers) need to become conscious of the signals sent to

students *via* body language, oral intonation, and other non-verbal types of communication. A judgmental sentiment is communicated verbally in a couple of seconds but with a raised eyebrow almost instantaneously. As teachers, we must endeavor to be accepting, inclusive, and non-judgmental. We also need to notice and understand our students' non-verbal language: Nervous smiles, pauses, and inquisitive glances all have meanings that require our interpretation; head position and voice inflection are not only culture-specific but gender-specific as well; and certain classroom patterns (such as who interrupts whom, when, how often, and under what circumstances) speak volumes about the real lines of social and sexual power that govern our students' behavior and learning potential. As teachers, we must learn to detect and ~ when necessary ~ redirect out of harmful range such forms of student communication.

3) Third, as their students' primary English language models, ESOL teachers must at all costs avoid the use of sexist and racist language themselves. Unfortunately, simple "good will towards men [sic]" will not suffice here; there are specific linguistic techniques that must be learned and used if the ESOL/EFL professional is to avoid this cardinal sin. In particular, the teacher needs to avoid ethnic and sexual generalization, the use of the so-called "generics", and sex-or-culture-specific stereotypical expressions (scattered throughout the very language we are trying to help students learn!). On the second item, we should note three vital desiderata: that the English language has no unique epicene third person singular pronoun ("singular they" being, of course, also plural), that the word "man" was once *but is no longer* a gender-neutral noun, and that this particular area of inclusive language is fraught with formidable editorial ~ and therefore pedagogical – difficulties.[3]

4) Fourth, and finally, teachers can only innovate comfortably in the classroom, without fear of relapsing into sexist stereotypes, if they will take the trouble to familiarize themselves with some of the literature on the subject of sexism and language. In the interests of facilitating that task, a *SELECT READING & USAGE LIST ON LANGUAGE AND SEXISM* is

appended to this article. It is offered, however, with a caveat: Male-favored English has been a millenium in the making; inclusive English has only recently begun its process of creation, and we are a long way from consensus on solutions to some of the problems that arise from our awareness of a need for language that is gender inclusive. In view of this, we must be careful not to preach certainty in instances where there is as yet none. Michael Newman says it just right:

> It only confuses beginning writers to be told to follow a rule where none exists. Simple injunctions: "use he", "avoid his or her", "pluralize antecedents", or even "use they" do not do justice to the problem writers face. It is far better to tell them the truth. The issue of which pronoun to use is not so much governed by syntactic rule as it is by meaning, and this meaning is embedded in a social context of gender relations.

What is true for pronominal usage is no less true for inclusive language as a whole, and therefore for every teacher and writer who wishes to be gender attentive. My personal wish is for that group to include all teachers and writers, and particularly all those who teach or learn to write in an ESOL/EFL classroom. Whether one is comfortable with it or not, gender sensitivity is the revolutionary and truly novel linguistic development of our age. As Richard Norris once observed:

> Alexander Pope could with a perfect and thoughtless innocence write: "Man never is, but always to be, blessed"; but when I read his words, I surreptitiously wonder if he meant women too. Of course he did; he just didn't mention them. But then that is precisely the point ....

NB: In 1992, this article appeared in a slightly different form in Vol. 2, #2 of "Working Papers on Language, Gender and Sexism", Monash University, Victoria, Australia.

ABOUT THE AUTHOR

Effie Papatzikou Cochran is an Associate Professor in the Department of English at John Jay College of Criminal Justice of the City University of New York. Her major fields of research are socio-linguistics and academic writing and grammar. Her special interests professionally include gender and language, bilingual and bidialectal code-switching, and theater-in-education. Her doctoral dissertation is on linguistic sexism and the pseudo-generic. Her article on Greek Diglossia appeared in the International Journal of the Sociology of Language in 1997. She is currently editing TESOL's volume on mainstreaming for "Case Studies in TESOL Practice".

REFERENCES

Abzug, Bella & Kelber, Mim (1984). Gender gap. Boston: Houghton Mifflin, 105-115.

Eakins, Barbara Westbrook & Eakins, R. Gene (1978). Definition by gender. In Sex differences in human communication. Boston: Houghton Mifflin, 114-125.

Gregersen, Edgar A. (1979). Sexual linguistics. In Orasanu, Judith, Slater, Mariam K., & Adler, Leonore Loeb, (eds.) Language, sex and gender (vol. 327 of the Annals of the New York Academy of Sciences). New York: New York Academy of Sciences, 3-19.

Hall, Roberta M. & Sandler, Bernice (1982). The classroom climate: A chilly one for women. Washington DC: Association of American Colleges.

Newman, Michael. The rules, the student, her pronouns, and their meaning. Unpublished; portions quoted by permission. A lengthier article on the same topic - Michael Newman (1992). Pronominal disagreements: The stubborn problem of singular epicene antecedents - has been published in vol. 21, #3 of Language in Society, London: Cambridge University Press.

Norris, Richard. "Inclusive" language and language about God. An unpublished conference paper delivered in the late 1980's.

Oates, Whitney J. & O'Neill, Eugene jr. (1938), eds. The complete Greek drama. New York: Random House, 2:1012-1013.

Sadker, Myra Pollack (1983). Sex bias in colleges and universities: The report card #2. Washington DC: American University, Mid-Atlantic Center for Sex Equity (10 pp.).

Sadker, Myra Pollack & Sadker, David Miller (1985). Sexism in the schoolroom of the 80's. Psychology Today, March, 54-57.

Thorne, Barrie & Henley, Nancy (1975), eds. Language and sex: Difference and dominance. Rowley MA: Newbury House. See also the papers in Thorne, Kramarae, & Henley's 1983 volume cited in the select reading & usage list following.

Trudgill, Peter (1983). Language and sex. In Sociolinguistics: An introduction. Middlesex, England: Penguin Books, 78-99.

A SELECT READING & USAGE LIST ON LANGUAGE AND SEXISM

Baron, Dennis (1986). Grammar and gender. New Haven: Yale University Press.

Bolinger, Dwight (1980). Language the loaded weapon. London: Longman.

Corbett, Greville (1991). Gender. London: Cambridge University Press.

Farb, Peter (1974/1979). Word play: What happens when people talk? New York: Alfred A. Knopf / Bantam.

Frank, Francine & Anshen, Frank (1983). Language and the sexes. Albany: State University of New York Press.

Gilligan, Carol (1982). In a different voice: Psychological theory and women's development. Cambridge MA: Harvard University Press.

Henley, Nancy M. (1977). Body politics: Power, sex, and nonverbal communication. Englewood Cliffs, NJ: Prentice-Hall.

Key, Mary Ritchie (1975). Male/female language. Metuchen, NJ: The Scarecrow Press.

Klein, Susan S. (1985), ed. Handbook for achieving sex equity in education. Baltimore: The Johns Hopkins University Press.

Kramarae, Cheris & Treichler, Paula A. (1985). A feminist dictionary. Boston, MA: Pandora.

Lakoff, Robin (1975). Language and women's place. New York: Harper & Row.

Miller, Casey & Swift, Kate (1977). Words and women. Garden City, NY: Anchor/Doubleday.

Nilsen, Alleen Pace, Bosmajian, Haig; Gershuny, H. Lee; & Stanley, Julia P. (1977). Sexism and language. Urbana, IL: National Council of Teachers of English.

Orasanu, Judith et al. Language, sex and gender (see under Gregersen in references above).

Penfield, Joyce (1987), ed. Women and language in transition. Albany: State University of New York Press.

Tannen, Deborah (1986/1991). That's not what I meant! New York: William Morrow / Ballantine.

_____ (1990). You just don't understand. New York: Ballantine.

Thorne, Barrie, Kramarae, Cheris, & Henley, Nancy (1983). Language, gender and society. Rowley, MA: Newbury House. See also the papers in Thorne & Henley's 1975 volume listed under references above.

STYLE AND INSTRUCTIONAL MANUALS

Frank, Francine Wattman & Treichler, Paula A. (1989). Language, gender, and professional writing: Theoretical approaches and guidelines for nonsexist usage. New York: The Modern Language Association of America, Commission on the Status of Women in the Profession.

Hacker, Diana (1992). A writer's reference. New York: St. Martin's Press.

Maclin, Alice (1986). Reference guide to English: A handbook of English as a second language (2nd edition). New York: Holt, Rinehart and Winston.

Maggio, Rosalie (1991/1992). The bias-free word finder: A dictionary of nondiscriminatory language. Boston: Beacon.

McGraw Hill guidelines for bias-free publishing (1983). New York: McGraw Hill.

Miller, Casey & Swift, Kate (1988). The handbook of nonsexist writing (2nd edition). New York: Harper & Row (Barnes & Noble).

Pauwels, Anne (1991). Non-discriminatory language. Canberra: Australian Government Publishing Service.

Sadker, Myra Pollack & Sadker, David Miller (1982). Sex equity handbook for schools. New York: Longman.

Sorrels, Bobbye D. (1983). The nonsexist communicator: Solving the problems of gender and awkwardness in modern English. Englewood Cliffs, NJ: Prentice-Hall.

ENDNOTES

1. *Masculinus genus dignus est quam faemininum et faemininus quam neutrum* ("The masculine is a worthier gender than the feminine, [just as the feminine is worthier] than the neuter.") was a common dictum in Latin grammars of the time, whence English grammarians derived the principle. Elizabeth S. Sklar discusses the matter in detail in her 1983 College English (vol. 45, pp. 348-358) article "Sexist Grammar Revisited", including the odd use of the form *"dignus"* (instead of the comparative *"dignior"* worthier).

2. In 1982 Roberta Hall and her colleagues at the Association of American Colleges produced a carefully researched and chilling summary of the obstacles faced by women in academia. Almost two decades later, despite significant progress in certain professional arenas and some advances in the academy, every one of the conditions reported by the Hall paper can still be found in today's college classrooms. Association of American Colleges publications are available from 1818 "R" Street, NW, Washington, DC 20009, telephone (202) 387-1300.

3. In a brilliant and delightful but unfortunately never published article ("The Rules, the Student, Her Pronouns, and Their Meaning"), Michael Newman leads his readers through the various pitfalls one encounters when trying to find appropriate pronouns for generic – or, more properly, epicene – antecedents. No solution is without its problems: "'Permissive' instructors who might be inclined to accept (singular) '*they*' must deal with the fact that many if not most of the future readers of their students' writing will consider it to be incorrect. Yet those who support some form of pronominal 'law and order' are being naive if they believe it is enough to tell students that the question is simply one of avoiding pronoun-antecedent disagreements. This approach of 'just say no' to antecedent-pronoun disagreement leaves students at risk either of being chastised for sexism or of getting lost in the maze of alternatives to epicene '*he*'." Newman's article in the present volume is in some respects an expansion of his earlier essay.

DISCIPLINING THE SCHOOLGIRL BODY

by
Barbara Kamler
Deakin University, Australia

ABSTRACT

This chapter examines everyday practices of schooling for the ways in which they discipline children to behave and think as girls and boys in school. Of particular interest is the centrality of the body to the process of gendering and the ways in which the process of bodily regulation works differently for girls and boys. A feminist poststructuralist analysis of language makes visible the way teacher talk, ritualized games, and songs promote gendered discourses despite the best intentions of teachers.

Early childhood classrooms are filled with song. Songs such as *The Dingle Dangle Scarecrow*, where children are encouraged to sing and move their bodies to the lyrics, were common fare in Mrs. T's Prep[1] (kindergarten) classroom.

TEXT 1

The Dingle Dangle Scarecrow

When all the cows were sleeping and the sun had gone to bed,
Up jumped the scarecrow and this is what he said,
"I'm a dingle dangle scarecrow with a flippy floppy hat,
I can shake my hands like this and shake my feet like that."

When all the hens were roosting and the moon behind the cloud,
Up jumped the scarecrow and shouted very loud,
"I'm a dingle dangle scarecrow with a flippy floppy hat,
I can shake my hands like this and shake my feet like that."

---

[1] In Victoria (Australia), the first year of school is referred to as "Prep"; in other Australian states as "Kindergarten" (New South Wales) or "Reception" (South Australia).

While it is usual to view classroom songs as innocent fun, this chapter analyzes the multiple purposes such songs serve, the discourses they mobilize, and the gendered positionings they accomplish. It argues that *The Dingle Dangle Scarecrow* is not simply a form of entertainment to keep children amused, but works, in conjunction with other texts in Mrs. T's Prep classroom, to regulate children's bodies into the schoolgirls and schoolboys they become. For after all, the "dingle dangle scarecrow" is the only figure in the song with agency, and he is identified as male. His female defined counterparts - the cows and hens - are by contrast, inactive. The cows are sleeping and the hens are exercising their biological imperative to roost, but it is the scarecrow the children are asked to identify with. They become the scarecrow (*I'm a dingle dangle scarecrow*); they shake their hands and feet as he would and give voice to his words, suggesting perhaps, that a song of childhood is not necessarily a song of innocence.

The use of song and ritual to control and shape children's bodies was a pervasive characteristic of Mrs. T's interactions with the young children in her care. Drawing on Bourdieu's (1977) notion of *habitus*, such everyday practices of schooling can be examined for the ways in which they "structure in" to children's bodies and minds enduring ways of behaving and thinking as girls and boys in school. The process of shaping the student *habitus* will be referred to as "disciplinary work", using Foucault's (1979) notion of the "internalization of the gaze" of authority to produce social power relations (Foucault 1979). Disciplinary work is designed to help children learn how to be pupils in relation to school society, rather than helping them learn about new content areas. Of particular interest is the centrality of the body to the process of gendering and the ways in which the process of bodily regulation works differently for girls and boys.

This chapter examines the teacher talk, games, and songs, in Mrs. T's Prep classroom, and the ways in which these discipline the schoolgirl body to achieve the work of the institution, where children will remain for half of their compulsory formal education. It resists, however, producing the kind of genre where researchers scrutinise teacher words for their failings and use these as prescriptions for what teachers should do. Rather, we would point out that Mrs. T's position as a teacher under scrutiny was an extremely difficult one. Her generosity in allowing access to her classroom and herself was indicative of a deep personal commitment to gender equity. There is little sense in which she received any of the personal and professional rewards that pertain to much classroom ethnographic or action-research involving more interactive, collaborative participation with the researchers. Rather, she "subjected" herself to an intensity of scrutiny that very few of us writing and reading this chapter will ever experience, and that now leaves her, in representation, open to intense scrutiny and interpretation.

THE CONTEXT OF THE STUDY

The song and other texts examined in this chapter come from a Gender Equity Curriculum Reform Project (B. Kamler, R. Maclean, J. Reid, and A. Simpson 1994; see also Kamler 1999 for further analyses of the data from this project) in which we examined the experience of girls and boys as they enter the first month of their first year of primary school. The beginning of formal schooling has been acknowledged as a significant time of induction into the culture of formal schooling. It is the assumption of our study, however, that the construction of gender begins from the very first moment children enter the institutional field of discourse and action that makes up schooling. We acknowledge the valuable and interesting work that has already been undertaken with reference to the kindergarten setting (Davies 1989, Willes 1981, Fernie *et al* 1992, Corsaro, 1988), but shift focuses quite consciously away from the early childhood emphasis of this earlier work to an analysis of the discursive and bodily practices that characterize "starting school" for some Australian children in the nineties.

Our research adopted case study methodology to focus on one class group of twenty-eight Prep children entering a suburban primary school in a large regional centre in southern Victoria. The school drew on a population from a middle-lower socioeconomic area consisting of diverse multicultural origins, including Serbian, Croatian, Greek, Japanese, Sri Lankan, and Chinese. The classroom and playground experience of these children was observed and recorded on videotape, audiotape, and in field notes kept by the research team over a period of four and a half school weeks in January and February 1993, that is, the first four weeks of the Australian school year. Picture books, videotapes, pictures, audiotapes, and worksheets presented to the children were recorded or duplicated. At least two of the four members of the research team were present at all times during the study, and an outside, professional team of video and sound recordists was present one day each week. In this way, we hoped to compile as detailed and multifaceted a representation of the practices that comprise the first month of school as possible.

The values and visions that have informed this research can be described as indicative of a feminist poststructuralist position. The subject positioning of the school-girl in relation to her sense of self and others is neither a unitary nor a received identity. It is not put on with a blue-and-white-checked school uniform, or marked and measured with checks and crosses. Rather, as Valerie Walkerdine notes, it is produced as "a nexus of subjectivities, in relations of power which are constantly shifting", so that the school-girl is rendered "at one moment powerful and at another powerless" (Walkerdine 1981, p. 14) as she works to construct her identity as one of this new social group. In poststructuralist terms, the subject is *always* precarious, contradictory and "in process"; therefore its essence cannot be captured for presentation here, or anywhere.

However, we take from the perspective of feminist poststructuralism the assumption that school-girl subjectivities do not necessarily *have* to be distinctively structured in the way they currently are. Jane Flax reminds us that:

If subjectivity is constituted by pregiven categories like "masculine" or "feminine", no individual subject can escape the effects of these categories any more than s/he could speak a private language. Unless the entire discursive field (and each subject's unconscious) is changed, these categories will continue to generate particular forms of subjectivity beyond the control of individuals, no matter how freely the subject believes s/he is playing with them. (Flax 1992, p. 455)

Bronwyn Davies calls this the "incorrigibility" of the male-female dualism in our society (Davies 1989). She shows how as children we learn the discursive and bodily practices that constitute us differentially as *either* female *or* male as we learn our language and social practice. This is because our interactions with and representations of these are based on a seemingly "natural", but demonstrably contrived, bipolarization. The feminist work towards upsetting and challenging the male/female dualism within the existing school structures remains an important function of educational research and of our own study. This project can be regarded in these terms as critically pragmatic, as "showing and telling" school practices in such a way that they are made strange enough to warrant a questioning consideration of their naturalness and normality, and so that they can be read as discursive constructs rather than as presentations of reality.

THE ANALYTICAL FRAME

Our research approached the analysis of gender by combining critical linguistic with feminist poststructuralist analyses. This is not necessarily an easy synthesis, as linguistics is rarely situated within the wider social and political concerns of gender politics, and poststructuralism rarely incorporates linguistic analyses of specific language texts as part of its tradition. Nevertheless, it is useful to work at both levels, combining the insights of theorists such as Michel Foucault (1977) and Chris Weedon (1987) with text analytic traditions within systemic linguistics (Halliday 1985) and critical linguistic studies (Kress 1985, Fairclough 1992). Our work can be located within an emerging corpus of Australian studies which also explores the relationship between discourse in a poststructuralist formulation and the specificity of language choices made in particular sites, such as school (see, for example, the special issue of *Discourse*, Critical Discourse Analysis in Educational Settings 1997).

Discourse is a term used by both social theorists (e.g. Foucault 1972) and linguists (e.g. Kress 1985, Fairclough 1992). From a linguistic perspective, referring to language as discourse signals an intention to investigate it as a form of social practice. Discursive practice is manifested linguistically in the form of texts, using text in Michael Halliday's (1985) sense to include both spoken and written language use. We can analyse the features of text as traces or cues of the discourses operating, making the distinction here between text and discourse, central in Linda Brodkey's work. "We read and write (and speak) texts, not discourses - at least my understanding of poststructural theory tells me to examine texts for traces of discourse or discourses" (Brodkey 1992, p. 303).

As texts are always enmeshed within a range of social attitudes, values, and assumptions about gender relations, an analysis of texts can make visible the discourses operating and the part they play in constructing gendered subjectivities. A detailed examination of the way discursive practices operate on a moment by moment basis during the first month of school can identify ways in which language actually functions to both privilege and marginalize a variety of gendered subject positions within the new school culture.

Even the best linguistic analyses, however, are not sufficient for making sense of lived experience in classrooms. Being a researcher in Mrs. T's Prep classroom confronted us with what Terry Threadgold (1992, p. 9) calls the "role of embodied subjectivity in the making of all texts". Watching the new Prep students struggle to negotiate and hold on to interim positions of power foregrounded the centrality of the body to the process of gendering and challenged us to develop a method of analysis that attended carefully to both the visual and linguistic. Michel Foucault's work has been particularly helpful here in offering a central emphasis on discourse as a form of power which both literally and metaphorically inscribes the collective and individual social body. Discourse, as Elizabeth Grosz (1990, p. 63) suggests, operates not as an abstract set of ideas but as "a material series of processes", where power actively marks bodies as social, and inscribes them, as an effect of this marking, with differentiated "attributes of subjectivity".

SONGS OF DISCIPLINE

The Dingle Dangle Scarecrow song, with which this chapter begins, was sung during the first hour of school on February 3, and was one of eight songs sung during the first 40 minutes of the day. The diagram below sets out the order and location of these songs, with numbers indicating the passage of minutes within the first hour.

1.30   Ciao bon giorno

2.00   Ciao bon giorno (reprise)

3.20   How many fingers on my hand (finish 5.07)

5.49   Stand Up. Move to Circle for Morning News

6.00   I'm a little teapot

7.32   Sit Down for Morning News
       (*12 students share news*)

18.10 Dingle Dangle Scarecrow
       (*13 students share news*)

33.40 Hands on heads

34.50 Following directions at seats

39.50 Return to Rug

40.30 Incy Weency Spider

40.52 Roll Over

41.30 Twinkle Twinkle

This segment of morning activity shows Mrs. T using three songs to focus the children's attention. After a long session of morning news and "direction games", she again uses three songs to mark the end of the 40 minute segment, before moving the children to a new seatwork activity where they will identify their names and trace over them.

The Dingle Dangle Scarecrow occurs in the midst of morning news and serves as an orchestrated interruption. February 3 was the first formal news session of the year, where every child in the circle is given the chance to speak. With 25 children present, it took 26 minutes to move around the circle so all children could have their turn. However, 40 minutes is a long time for five year old children to sit, and the children grew restless, their bodies squirming, and sprawling in a variety of body positions on the rug. Mrs. T thus interrupted the morning news with *The Dingle Dangle Scarecrow* to refocus their attention.

The fact that the first 40 minutes of the day are spent organizing, regulating, and arranging the children's bodies on the rug and at their seats signals something of the intensity with which the first month of school is directed at disciplining the student body before children can get to the "real work of school". The songs play a major role in this disciplining, where the central purpose of singing is not so much the rhythmic pleasure of song as much as the bodily discipline song can achieve.

This was quite different from the use of song the previous year, when we observed seventeen of the children in their Kindergarten classroom located across the street. When the Kindergarten teacher wanted to call the whole group together, she began a song as the signal for the group to gather on the rug. As children finished their activity and joined the whole group, one by one, the momentum and volume of the song grew. They then sang a series of well known, and judging from the smiling and laughter, well-loved songs. This was a communal time the goals of which appeared to be pleasure, community, and pleasure in community.

In Mrs. T's Prep classroom children also engaged in song

as a community, but the purpose seemed to shift (although the linguistic form stayed the same) to collective regulation, an invitation to discontinue private conversation and move their mouths together in unison. The singing was led by Mrs. T, who decided when and at what intervals the songs would occur and whose voice and gestures set the cadence, stress, and pitch.

The songs regulate by targeting the children's bodies. Most of the songs require the children to perform actions on their own bodies and to do so in unison. Hands are often the target in the forty minute segment. In *How many fingers on my hand,* the children count 1, 2, 3, 4, 5 fingers first on the left hand and then on the right; in *I'm a little teapot,* the children form their hands into the handle and spout of the teapot; in *Twinkle twinkle little star,* the children raise their hands above their heads and make their fingers into twinkling stars. In each instance, children are required to move their hands not only for the fun of the movement but to keep them off other children.

The Dingle Dangle Scarecrow song regulates larger body movements. The children are told to get in their box at the start of the song and with this signal they move down to the floor into a small ball. Only a few of the children actually sing with the teacher, but at the signal *Up jumped the scarecrow,* they jump up and all join in the chorus, *I can shake my hands like this, I can shake my feet like that.* They move down again onto the floor and repeat the cycle for the second verse, a bodily contraction, a jumping springing movement, then a shaking of the hands and feet, presumably ready then to sit down and pay attention to the twelve other children who have yet to give their morning news.

The songs are a routinized practice. Following Foucault's (1979) explanation of institutional regulation, the songs appear to operate as one of a number of systems of surveillance and regulation which are "inscribed at the heart of the practice of teaching, not as an additional or adjacent part, but as a mechanism that is inherent to it and which increases its efficiency" (Foucault 1979, p. 176).

Mrs. T was observed teaching the children only a few new songs during the first month of school and relied rather on songs already familiar from *Play School, Sesame Street*, and kindergarten the year before. Because little energy had to be expended on remembering new words, the songs could function more directly as regulating mechanisms in the first month of school.

BODY PARTS

During the first month of school, songs were most often preceded and followed by teacher talk which provided guidelines to students on how to produce the right body. Below *The Dingle Dangle Scarecrow* is recontextualized within the teacher talk surrounding it. Children are identified as "student" rather than by name when it is not possible to specify from the videotape who is actually speaking.

The Dingle Dangle Scarecrow
RECONTEXTUALIZED

1 2 3 4 5 6 7 8	Mrs.T	Everybody stand yourselves up for a little minute. Two feet together, shhhhh, do this quietly. Nice big stretch up tall, ohh dear, Mrs. T should be in bed I think and down again, give your shoulders a wriggle, now your head, very slowly, oh slowly, that's it just to wake us up. Right down you get in your boxes.
9	Student	What for?
10	Mrs. T	Right down.
11 12 13 14 15 16	Mrs.T & class	When all the cows are sleeping and the sun is in the sky, up jumped the scarecrow and this is what he said. "I'm a dingle dangle scarecrow with a flippy floppy hat, I can shake my hands like this and shake my feet like that."

| 17 | Mrs. T | Down you go again, down you go. |

18	Mrs. T & class	When all the hens are roosting and the
19		moon is in the sky, up jumped the
20		scarecrow and shouted very loud. "I'm a
21		dingle dangle scarecrow with a flippy
22		floppy hat, I can shake my hands like
23		this and shake my feet like that."

24	Mrs. T	OK guys, stand up nice and tall, come
25		on Jodie, stand up, mustn't talk,
26		tummies in, come on Con, up you get,
27		tummies in, two feet together,
28		shhhhhhhhh. I want your lips buttoned.

| 29 | Student | Ohhh. |

30	Mrs. T	Now sit down quietly, shh. You know I
31		forgot something, I was going to give
32		you people something, sit, sweetie, sit
33		over there. This morning I liked the way
34		that you walked in so quietly. I meant to
35		go and give you another yellow star, so
36		I'll give it to you now and so far we've
37		got three yellow stars on the board.
38		Maybe when we get to five yellow stars,
39		there might be something special, we'll
40		have to think about that, Con, could you
41		sit up nicely please, and Tom, you can
42		sit there but just sit quietly. Con, sit up
43		nicely, that's it. Right now remember
44		some of you people have forgotten the
45		rules, remember if someone is talking
46		do you all talk at the same time?

| 47 | Student | No, no no no. |

| 48 | Mrs. T | No, because why? Why don't you speak |
| 49 | | if someone else is speaking? |

| 50 | Student | Because. |

| 51 | Mrs. T | Because why? |

| 52 | Allan | (inaudible) |

53	Mrs. T	Well, that's one reason Allan, that's a
54		good reason. Does anybody else have
55		any other reasons why you might not
56		talk? Karen, Karen, I like the way you're
57		sitting up there beautifully with your
58		hand up.

59	Karen	'Cause it's wrong.
60	Mrs. T	Because, yes, because it's a bit wrong,
61		isn't it? Why is it a bit wrong do you
62		think, Thomas?
63	Thomas	Because it's rude.
64	Mrs. T	It is a bit rude, I find it a little bit rude; if
65		someone speaks when I'm speaking I
66		feel maybe it's just a little bit rude.
67	Student	(inaudible) And you just can't hear what
68		you're saying.
69	Mrs. T	That's right, OK, so where were we up
70		to? Sitting up very nicely, we're going to
71		get to all you people in a few minutes,
72		crossed legs.

Just prior to the song, Mrs. T gets the children to stand and stretch. The stated purpose is *just to wake us up,* (7), an innocent stretching time to move the body and help the children stay attentive to the morning news which will continue in a few moments. The lexical naming of the children's body parts, their *feet, shoulders,* and *heads* (2,5,6), occurs both here and at the conclusion of the song, where *tummies, feet,* and *lips* are named (26-28) and Mrs. T attempts to get the children focused, straightened, and ready to return to the morning news.

These injunctions about the arrangement and rearrangement of student bodies, as in *tummies in, two feet together, lips buttoned* regularly punctuate the first month of school and are typically realized by naming a variety of different body parts, including hands, lips, laps, eyes, noses, legs, arms, and feet, rather than referring to the whole child body. The body parts are most often located linguistically within a teacher command, realized in the imperative mood, as is evident in the following body targeting imperatives, which come from other portions of the morning on Feb. 3rd:

Hands to yourself please
Hands in your laps
Put up your hands
Crossed legs
I want to see all these legs crossed
I want your lips buttoned
Listen with your ears not your mouths
Look at me with your eyes so I know
You are listening to me
Can I have your eyes
OK guys, close the mouths

Posture, movement, and visual gaze are all monitored and directed through teacher imperatives. Mrs. T has the power to tell the children to move their bodies in particular ways, sometimes identifying herself as the source of the command through the pronominal *I* or *me*, other times not. The class is sometimes named as *everybody*, or *guys*, but more often not named. Their body parts, however, are named in the plural, through the pronominal *your*, although this shifts sometimes to a plural body part *the mouths*, belonging to the collective. It is less easy, however, to read at whom the imperatives are directed: the group or the individual? Are these the body parts belonging to one body or many? Which body is to respond? What appears to be happening here is the discursive construction of a collective student body, for as Mary Willes (1981) points out, every year it is the job of the teacher to get children moving as one classroom body.

Individual child bodies, new to the regimes of formal schooling, are thus being shaped by Mrs. T into a student body, twenty-seven individual squirming bodies are being linguistically and bodily constituted as one, to move as if with one pair of hands, one pair of legs, one mouth that can tolerate only one voice at a time, one back that is erect and attentive, nice and straight. The body parts need to be well disciplined so they do not kick; so they face the front, not the back, of the classroom; so they raise their collective hand for permission to speak or to go to the toilet. They are to be quiet and speak softly, to put their hands up and keep their hands in their own collective lap.

This construction of the collective student body, however, is not accomplished through a simple imposition of power from the teacher at the top to the children at the bottom. The teacher discourse positions the body as object, as an accumulation of named parts which needs to be surveilled. Mrs. T acts upon those objects and begins simultaneously to provide the language in which to read those actions. As Valerie Walkerdine (1987) points out, actions on objects don't make any sense without a discourse though which to read them. These ways of classifying and categorizing the body, and referring to its various parts, are put to work so that "they generate self-surveillance, wherein the subject internalizes the disciplinary and cultural gaze as her or his own" (Luke 1992, p. 111). What is of interest, as Allan Luke points out, is how Foucault's (1988) notion of the technologies of power, which govern the conduct of individuals, interact with technologies of self to permit individuals to act upon themselves and their own bodies.

Teacher evaluations attached to body postures certainly seem to play a role here, as exemplified by Mrs. T's talk to the children once they are seated again, following the scarecrow song (33-38). Here Mrs. T praises the group for walking. Her use of the pronominal *you* suggests the walking was accomplished as one body which will now be rewarded. The action of walking is itself not an action worthy of praise, but when done quietly and collectively is read by Mrs. T as worthy of yellow stars. Later in the year, presumably, stars will be awarded for academic work, but here in the first month of school the serious work is constituted as body regulation. There is an interesting shift here as well from the pronominal *I* to *we*, which works to position the children discursively as colluding in Mrs. T's evaluations. She is clearly the dispenser of stars and praise, *I was going to give, I liked the way, I meant to go, I'll give,* but when it comes to stars, it is *we* who are *getting* them and *thinking* about an extra special reward. This linguistic slippage between student and teacher subjectivity works to help students engage in self-surveillance.

While much of Mrs. T's evaluations are directed at the collective student body, individuals are also singled out and named, either for transgressing or for complying. It is through these naming practices (40-43) that some of the more overt gendering work is accomplished. Con and Tom are named as boys who have transgressed, who have not internalized the attributes of nicely and quietly. Although linguistically the teacher evaluations are not expressed as negative evaluations, but as an interrogative (*Could you sit up nicely?*) and an imperative (*Sit up nicely.*), they position the boys negatively as having bodies which are hard to control.

> Those who have not internalized the teacher's gaze, those who are not willing participants, are singled out... Where the technology of the self fails, the technology of power steps in. Where the gaze has not been internalized by the children, it is externally asserted by the teacher. (Luke 1992:120)

The pattern of externally asserting the gaze, however, is clearly gendered and girls are more often named for being willing subjects, for bodily obedience and compliance, as in *Karen, I like the way you're sitting up there beautifully with your hand up* (56-58). While boys are seen for *not sitting,* girls are seen for *sitting.* This does not mean that there are not also girls transgressing or boys complying. It does mean that such actions are often not seen or named by the teacher. Michelle, for example, a girl who is constituted through teacher talk as a good schoolgirl subject, engaged in a great deal of aggressive body action, kicking Tom and hitting Con on the head when he was lying down. She is never singled out or named, however, for such transgressions. It was not clear whether Mrs. T even saw her engaging in such acts, because the teacher gaze itself is constituted within the male-female dualisms, and what is seen and named is always partial, meaning both incomplete and interested.

To illustrate further how it is that bodily practices such as sitting become tied to pupil selection in gendered ways, it is useful to examine a story reading event later in the morning of February 3rd. Mrs. T had set up a book on the easel and was looking for someone to help her with the class story, to move the pointer on the words as they are read aloud by the class.

Perfect Sitting

1 2 3 4 5 6 7 8 9	Mrs. T	I'm looking for someone to help me, wonder who's sitting up very nice...Right now. Ellen, have you been sitting like that all that time? How did you get to be so perfect? Have you been practicing for years? You haven't, it just comes natural to you? Come up here and be my helper, anybody who sits up like that, guys, has just got to help me.
		[As the lesson proceeds Rohan is named for not listening.]
10 11 12 13	Mrs. T	I'm sorry but we have to read it again. Rohan, turn around. Let's read it again because Rohan missed out on the story. "Look I'm at school."
14 15 16 17 18 19 20 21 22 23	Mrs. T	Now let's have a little look here. I wonder if I can ask somebody, and I'm only going to ask those people who are sitting beautifully and I think, perhaps, oh gee, tricky tricky tricky, Rohan you're sitting up pretty nice now. Actually, how about coming up and seeing if you can find me the word that might say 'sssschoool'. I wonder if he's clever, Ellen, do you think so?

Here posture is overtly used as the criterion for choosing. Ellen is singled out from the collective body and praised for her sitting (3-7). She is positioned by teacher discourse within the male-female binaries. Sitting nicely is equated with being perfect (5), and this comes naturally to Ellen (6), ostensibly because she is a girl. She is defined as "natural" within the preconstructed binaries and is marked as working within the feminine. Anyone who sits like girls gets to help the teacher (7-9). The good schoolgirl subjectivity thus becomes an extension of the female teacher subjectivity and gaze. Ellen is chosen to stand near the teacher, to hold the pointer of the teacher, and face the children. She is rewarded by being allowed to take on the gaze directly as teacher.

Her performance stands in direct contrast to Rohan, who is clearly not perfect. He is *pretty nice* (19). He/his body still needs to be disciplined; the teacher gaze must stay firmly on him. Ellen, the perfect sitter, is asked to take on teacher subjectivity and maintain that gaze externally. Perfect sitting becomes invested with moral regulation, and Ellen is invited to take on the teacher judgment and decide if Rohan is clever or not. *I wonder if he's clever Ellen do you think so?* (21-23). This type of gender regulation through posture, repeated hundreds of times during the first month in incidental, invisible ways, has real effects not only on children's bodies, but on their thoughts and ways of being. As Bourdieu (1990, p. 73) puts it, "What is 'learned by the body' is not something that one has, like knowledge that can be brandished, but something that one is."

HANDS ON HEADS

It is dangerous to focus solely on teacher talk and select data to demonstrate how technologies of power play a part in the representation and reproduction of gendered subjectivities, dangerous because it constructs an overly neat and simple picture. It is not the case that teachers impose discipline and children simply comply. Disciplinary power is not unitary any more than the subjectivities of the children who are in the process of becoming schoolgirls and schoolboys. Further, it is important to remember that transcripts of classroom events are themselves only a construction, and a partial one at that. The transcripts presented thus far clearly privilege a linguistic rather than a visual representation. They attend only to teacher and student words and ignore the embodied responses and actions of the children being regulated. Such omissions construct a fiction —an overly innocent world, where teachers control and children comply— where everyone is engaged in the same regulating activity at the same time.

To make more complex this analysis of disciplining, a final instance of body regulation from the morning of February 3rd is examined, with the body written into the transcript. In representing this session of *Hands on Heads*, a version of *Simon Says*, the teacher imperatives are placed in the left column and the corresponding actions of two children, Jodie and Tom, in the right column. This itself is a selection. Twenty five children participated in this "game", yet the transcript focuses on the way two children responded and resisted. This occurs not only because we found their interaction is fascinating, but because the video camera was focused on them. In setting out the transcript, the children's actions are aligned with the teacher talk to highlight the relationship between what the teacher says and what some of the children actually do.

Hands on Heads

1	Mrs. T	Could we please	Jodie crosses circle to
2		have Amy, Nikola?	move beside Tom.
3		Could you just stick	Jodie pushes Tom away.
4		Amy over there for me	Tom pushes Jodie.
5		please? That's it,	
6		and then she	
7		can keep an eye on	Jodie moves to push
8		what we're doing.	Tom.
9		Stand tall, Jodie.	Jodie moves away from Tom back across the circle where she began.
10		Hands on heads,	Jodie returns to Tom,
11		hands on shoulders,	hands out, tongue out.
12		hands ohh, hands	
13		behind backs, hands	
14		on knees, gee, some	Tom pushes Jodie.
15		of you are very quick,	
16		but I'm quicker. I'll	
17		trick you, hands on	
18		feet.	
19		Hands on elbows.	Tom pushes Ayse who returns from toilet.
20		Are you right there	Mrs. T pulls Ayse closer
21		Ayse?	to her.
22		Hands on nose.	Tom squeezes the back of Jodie's neck.

23	Hands on lips.	Tom pushes Jodie's back.
24 25	Hands on eyes, hands on ears.	Tom stamps his foot.
26 27	Hands on heads, tricky one.	Jodie points to Tom's foot.
28	Hands behind head	Tom puts his foot on Jodie's foot.
29 30	Mmm, very good, I didn't trick anybody.	Tom taps his foot on Jodie's, then exerts pressure. She opens her mouth as if to yell.
31	Hands on feet, Tom.	
32 33	Hands on feet, hands on knees.	Jodie and Tom both bend down to touch feet.
34	Hands behind backs.	Tom pokes his finger into Jodie's shoulder.
35	Hands in front.	Jodie and Tom stare at one another, she stands up, he remains crouched.
36 37 38	Hands on shoulders, hands on hips, where's your hips?	
39 40 41 42	Hands on shoulders Hands on elbows, stand nice and tall, arms by your side.	Tom pulls Jodie's shorts. Tom pulls Jodie's shorts again.
43 44	Do you know what I think Tom?	Tom stands up. Jodie watches.
45	Sshh, shh, shh.	Jodie points across the circle.
46 47 48 49 50 51 52 53 54 55	Do you know what I really think, I think there are some people in here who really need some practice in listening, because when I say something they don't always hear what I'm saying. So listen very	Tom moves across the circle away from Jodie to stand beside Benjamin and the boys.

56	carefully, I want you
57	to go and stand
58	behind a chair, off
59	you go.

Although Mrs. T presents Hands on Heads as a game, this is a childhood game again being transformed into a technology of regulation, which Mrs. T will be able to call on during the course of the day, the month, the year to regulate the children's behavior.

Linguistically, the imperative *hands on heads* has been shortened or ellipsed from *put your hands on your heads*, the actual command *put* is omitted, the *hands* are thematised or come first, and the pronominal *your* is omitted so that the individual *heads* of the children become a singular collective target, *head*. The effect of this is to shift the focus to the children's hands and away from both the instruction itself, *put*, and the person who is telling the children to move their bodies in prescribed ways, Mrs. T. This linguistic transformation can be diagramed as follows:

Mrs. T says: Put your hands on your heads
(Becomes) ⇒ **Put your hands on head**
(Becomes) ⇒ **Hands on Head**

Linguistically, then, the children ostensibly have agency, or rather their hands do, to act upon their own bodies, another instance of how technologies of power interact with technologies of self to produce self-surveillance. Writing in the actions of Jodie and Tom alongside the teacher imperatives, however, reveals that such body disciplining is not simply taken up by the children and internalized. The visual representation of bodies in *Hands on Heads*, in fact, allows us to produce more complex readings, whereby *Hands on Heads* is transformed into a different game we might call *Hands on Jodie*.

Valerie Walkerdine (1981) notes that gendered relations of power and resistance are continually reproduced in the classroom, in continual struggle and constantly shifting. Here alongside the authorized teacher talk, we see Tom producing actions with his hands, as he is being commanded, but resistantly. Powerless within the domain of the teacher discourse, he positions Jodie and Ayse as powerless subjects of other discourses of masculinist violence. He shoves Ayse as she returns to the circle (19) and targets a number of Jodie's body parts, including her neck (22), her back (23), her foot (28-30), her shoulder (34), and even the more taboo area covered by her shorts (39-42). Although Tom is not a physically grown man, he can take the position of men through his actions on girls' bodies. His power is gained by refusing to be constituted as the powerless subject in the teacher discourse and recasting the girls as the powerless subject of his.

It is not the case, however, that Jodie simply accepts this positioning. She is the one, after all, who moves towards Tom in the first place. Although she returns momentarily to her initial place in the circle after being named by Mrs. T (9), she returns buoyantly, hands on hips, tongue out, almost daring Tom. Significantly, Tom is positioned in the circle between Bianca and Alice, two of the girls Jodie likes to spend time with. She may in fact move in order to sit near her friends and displace Tom to make a space for herself. Although she endures physical abuse from Tom, she remains an active participant and in the end Tom does leave the space. Jodie points in the direction of the boys (45) and Tom moves back across the circle to stand with Benjamin and the others (46-49) as she takes her "rightful place" beside Bianca and Alice.

An important effect of this power struggle is the way in which Mrs. T interprets Tom's actions to lessen their oppressive effect. It is not clear, in fact, what she sees, as her attention is also directed at the twenty-three other children present on this day. The first time she polices the disturbance, she names Jodie as the perpetrator, *Stand tall, Jodie* (9), although Tom has been centrally involved in the pushing. When Tom shoves Ayse with some force, it is Ayse, the victim, who is named, *Are you right there Ayse?* (20-21), rather than Tom, the perpetrator of the violence. When Tom is finally named (31), after he more obviously stamps his foot on Jodie's, the reprimand is realized linguistically through the imperative of the game *Hands on feet, Tom*. Tom's resistance is thus seamlessly incorporated back into the domain of the teacher discourse where he is less powerful. He is not reprimanded for what he has done, and his violence remains, unnamed, just a normal part of classroom life.

At the conclusion Tom is again named, *Do you know what I think, Tom?* (43-44), but it is unclear whether Mrs. T is dissatisfied primarily with his performance or the whole group's, as she names *some people* and *they* (48-53) as the offenders, the ones who don't listen, who *don't always hear what I'm saying* (53-55). Mrs. T then initiates a further session of body regulation (55-59), where the children will be directed to stand behind, in front of, on and under the chairs, taking steps forward and backward to see if this time they can listen more carefully and get their bodies right.

Constructing the transcript with the teacher imperatives on the left and the child actions on the right, highlights the fact that in this interaction it is Mrs. T who controls the verbal domain. She talks, she speaks into existence a regime of regulation. The children do not speak, but to the extent that they mobilize resistance this occurs in the nonverbal domain, through the body. Thus it is that both the regulating and the resisting occur through bodily practices. This is not to say that the teacher's words do not have real effect. They target and surveil the body, limiting the range of subject positions made available to children. Subjectivity, however, as Walkerdine (1987, p. 10) points out, is "not simply produced within single texts, but at the intersection of competing discourses and practices".

This session of *Hands on Heads* suggests that while teacher discourse is a form of power which inscribes the collective student body, the process of inscription is itself a struggle. While Mrs. T's discourse positions the children's bodies as objects, the discourses of masculinity mobilized by Tom's actions target Jodie's body as object, and the discourses of femininity and female bonding mobilized by Jodie's actions compete with Tom's for supremacy. Without the visual representation of Jodie and Tom, it would be possible to read these children, and the 23 others not discussed, as simply submitting to school imposed disciplinary power. Such an analysis demonstrates, therefore, the importance of reading the embodied text rather than the linguistic text alone, and of utilizing more complex frames for reading children's actions than are currently available to teachers in many classrooms.

CONCLUSION

This chapter has attempted to make visible some of the seamless ways in which everyday school practices operate to discipline the student body. In his conceptualization of "kindergarten as academic bootcamp", Harry Gracey (1962) notes that learning to live by the routines of school appears to be the principal content of the student role. Such notions are confirmed by this analysis of the set of ritualized songs, games, and routines put in place in Mrs. T's classroom during the first month of school.

While it was clearly Mrs. T's purpose to teach the children systems of rules and control, it was *not* her intention to construct gendered subjectivities through such practices. Mrs. T is a teacher who adopted gender inclusive classroom practice and resisted constructing maternal domestic discourses typical of early childhood classrooms. Nevertheless, in certain situations, such as the disciplining practices examined in this chapter, she appears powerless to resist the gendering of her classroom discourse, because she is herself subject to powerful discourses and acts unwittingly and against her own stated intentions to reproduce both the discourse and its effects within her own social space.

Such contradictory practices raise serious problems about disciplining children's bodies in particular, and equitable schooling in general. While it is commonly accepted that children need to be regulated in some manner if they are going to be schooled, how this is done is at issue. The fact that the process of regulation appears to be so deeply and yet invisibly gendered needs serious consideration by the teaching and research communities. If teacher discourse continues to reproduce gendered meanings out of "habit", official discourses of gender equity and reform will be contradicted and undermined. It is clear that teachers need an increased awareness of the ways in which the discursive and bodily practices of schooling constitute children differentially as *either* female or male. Work with teachers that develops a discourse for examining subjectivity and the discursive forces which shape classroom talk would appear to be essential (see, for example, Kamler 1999). Without a way of making visible the gendered and contradictory ways we interact with children as schoolgirls and schoolboys from the very beginning of school, it is difficult to envisage transformation.

ABOUT THE AUTHOR

Barbara Kamler is an Associate Professor in Education at Deakin University. She has teaching and research interests in gendered language practices, writing pedagogy, critical literacies, and critical discourse analysis. She has published widely on issues of language and schooling across a variety of educational levels (elementary, secondary, university) and disciplines (education, English, law). Her recent books include Constructing Gender and Difference: Critical Research Perspectives on Early Childhood (1999 Hampton Press) and Relocating the Personal: A Critical Writing Pedagogy (2001 SUNY Press).

REFERENCES

Bourdieu, Pierre (1990). *The Logic of Practice.* (trans. Richard Nice). Cambridge: Polity Press.

Brodkey, Linda (1987). Writing critical ethnographic narratives. *Anthropology and Education* 18:2, 67-76.

Brodkey, Linda (1992). Articulating poststructural theory in research on literacy. In R. Beach, J.L. Green, M.L. Kamil & T. Shanahan (eds) *Multidisciplinary perspectives on literacy research.* Urbana, ILL: NCRE & NCTE, 293-318.

Corsaro, William (1988). Peer culture in the preschool. *Theory and Practice,* Vol. 127 (1) 19-24.

Fairclough, Norman (1992). *Discourse and social change.* Cambridge: Polity Press.

Flax, Jane (1992). The end of innocence. In Judith Butler and Joan W. Scott (eds.), *Feminists Theorize the Political.* New York and London: Routledge, 445-463.

Fernie, David, Davies, Bronwyn, Kantor, Rebecca, and McMurray, Paula (1992). *Becoming a person in the preschool: Creating integrated gender, school culture and peer culture positioning.* Unpublished manuscript in preparation, Ohio University.

Foucault, Michel (1977). *Language, counter-memory, practice.* Oxford: Basil Blackwell.

Foucault, Michel (1979). *Discipline and Punish.* New York: Harper.

Gracey, Harry (1962). Learning the student role: Kindergarten as academic boot camp. In H.R. Stub (ed.) *The sociology of education: A source book, 3rd ed.* Ill: Dorsey Press.

Grosz, Elizabeth (1990). Inscriptions and body-maps: Representations and the corporeal. In Terry Threadgold and Anne Cranny-Francis (eds) *Feminine, masculine and representation*. Sydney: Allen & Unwin, 62-74.

Halliday, M.A.K.(1985). *Introduction to functional grammar*. London: Edward Arnold.

Kamler, Barbara (1993). Constructing gender in the process writing classroom. *Language Arts*, 70 (2), 20-28.

Kamler, Barbara, Maclean, Rod, Reid, Joanne and Simpson, Alyson, (1994). *Shaping up nicely: The formation of schoolgirls and schoolboys in the first month of school*. Report for Gender Equity Curriculum Reform Project, Department of Education, Employment and Training, Canberra, ACT.

Kamler, Barbara, Comber, Barbara, Cook, Jackie (eds.) (1997). *Discourse: Special Issue, Critical Discourse Analysis in Educational Settings*, 18(3).

Kamler, Barbara (ed). (1999). *Constructing gender and difference: Critical research perspectives on early childhood*. Cresskill, NJ: Hampton Press.

Kress, Gunther (1985). *Linguistic processes in sociocultural practice*. Geelong, Vic: Deakin University Press.

Luke, Allan (1992). The body literate: Discourse and inscription in early literacy training. *Linguistics and Education*, 4, 107-129.

Reid, Joanne, Kamler, Barbara, Simpson, Alyson, Maclean, Rod (1994, in press). 'Do you see what I see': Reading a different classroom scene. *International Journal of Qualitative Studies in Education*.

Threadgold, Terry (1992). *Performing genre: Violence, the making of protected subjects, and the discourses of critical literacy and radical pedagogy*. Plenary paper International Domains of Literacy Conference, London Institute of Education, London University, Sept. 1992.

Walkerdine, Valerie (1987). Surveillance, subjectivity and struggle: Lessons from pedagogic and domestic practices. *CHS Occasional papers No. 11*, University of Minnesota.

Walkerdine, Valerie (1981). Sex, power and pedagogy. *Screen Education* 38, Spring, 14-24.

Willes, Mary (1981). Children becoming pupils: A study of discourse in nursery and reception classes. In Clem Adelman (ed.), *Uttering muttering: Collecting, using and reporting talk for social and educational research*, London, Grant McIntyre, 51-68.

Weedon, Chris (1987). *Feminist Practice and Poststructuralist Theory*. Oxford: Basil Blackwell.

Gender and Classroom Research:
WHAT'S SPECIAL ABOUT THE LANGUAGE CLASSROOM?

by

Jane Sunderland

Lancaster University, United Kingdom

ABSTRACT

The article discusses ESL/EFL classroom research on gender and its implications. Although a great deal of work has been done on gender in classrooms, including teacher-student and student-student talk, relatively little has been done in the second or foreign language classroom. What is "special" about a foreign language class is investigated here, looking in particular at subject matter, the role of the teacher and distribution of talking time, topics and materials, attitudes and apparent ability, and language learners' identity, and at what all these features may have to do with gender. The author hypothesizes that the language classroom, often considered a "girls' world", may be an easier learning domain for female than for male students. Although the findings are apparently positive for females, the reader should be aware that any finding which seems to favor females may, in fact, just be favoring students of higher ability.

INTRODUCTION

Though the era of "exposing" gender differences is over in research on gender in the classroom, the classroom itself remains an important epistemological site for gender research. The focus of this chapter is the contribution of the curricular subject to the genderedness of classrooms, and the implications of this contribution for research. The curricular subject in question is a language which is not the learners' mother tongue, known variously (and problematically) as a second / foreign / additional language, but here henceforth referred to simply as a "language". (*For a more general review of issues of language and gender in second and foreign language education, see Sunderland* [2000a]).

The questions I would like to explore in this article are:

- *What is special about the language classroom?*

- *What may this have to do with gender?*

- *What are the implications of this relationship for:*
  - (a) *Language classroom research questions in general.*
  - (b) *Research questions on gender in the language classroom in particular.*

- *What gender issues are specific to language classroom research?*

- *What classroom research issues are specific to gender?*

I will illustrate the discussion with examples from my own (1996) study of a "German as a Foreign Language classroom".

1. What is special about the language classroom?

Clearly, much of what happens in classrooms in general will be relevant to the language classroom, and language classroom research can therefore benefit from findings obtained in other subject classrooms. However, language classrooms may also have some special features (as may any subject classroom), and it is these I am concerned with here. In addition, several studies have found that gender effects varied with the subject (e.g. Leinhardt *et al.* [1979] found that teachers made more academic contact with girls in reading and boys in math). It is therefore possible not only that language classrooms are "special" in some way, but also that some of these special features have to do with gender.

Language classrooms themselves are extremely heterogeneous, along several dimensions. In particular, some students learn a "foreign" language which they do not see any opportunity of using with native speakers of that language; others study the dominant language of the country where they live, which they may not speak at home. Still others learn a language for a specific purpose, for example, to help them in business (e.g. "ESP" - English for Specific Purposes). Different purposes for learning - official as well as those coming from students' personal agendas - all help shape what the class is like[1]. The resultant heterogeneity means that some language classrooms will have a great deal in common with non-language classes: advanced EFL classes may look to an outsider like literature classrooms, for example; hands-on ESP classes may look like science classes. Nevertheless, there may be a "residual" set of common characteristics which language classes have a tendency to share.

These characteristics concern, I suggest:

(1) Language use
(2) The role of the teacher and distribution of talking time
(3) Topics and materials
(4) Attitudes and apparent ability
(5) Learners' identity.

1.1 Language use: since the subject matter is a second or foreign language, typically more than one language can be found in the language classroom

The *sine qua non* of the foreign/second language classroom is that a language is used that is not the students' first language. Accordingly, the most salient feature of the language classroom may be, typically, that at least two languages can be found there. This is likely to be the case even when teachers say they teach the target language in, and only in, the target language. Since the teacher may not be a native speaker of the target language, this raises the interesting possibility that a given student, because of his or her background, may perform better in the subject matter of the lesson (the target language) than the teacher does. It is hard to envisage this in other subject classrooms.

1.2 The role of the teacher and distribution of talking time: there is typically proportionally more speaking than in most other subject classrooms

One of the consequences of "communicative" language teaching has been the increasing importance of speaking as a skill in its own right (indeed, to many language teachers, "communicative" means "speaking"). Peck (1988) identifies "oral practice" as one of five "macro activities" basic to language teaching. Language teaching thus differs from subjects in which speaking is seen largely as a means to an end (for example, when the teacher asks questions in order to assess students' level of understanding). The language teacher may then try to decrease her or his own talking time (67% of all classroom talking time, in the conventional wisdom) in the interests of facilitating speaking opportunities on the part of the students, i.e. to increase the amount of their talk. In many settings, this is frequently done using pair- and groupwork, but the teacher may also try to achieve it in "whole-class" work, through frequent selection of students and/or self-selection by students.

Research indicates that the resultant distribution of student talking-time has a great deal to do with gender. Though overall student-talking time may be increased, numerous studies have suggested that this tends to be boy-talking rather than girl-talking time (Kelly 1988, Leder 1987, Swann and Graddol 1988, Sadker and Sadker 1985, Gilbert 1992, Jenkins and Cheshire 1990). In the case of teacher-selection, this appears to be not so much a matter of teacher-favoritism as a result of "joint collaboration" (French and French 1984, Swann and Graddol 1988). Further, especially in the case of whole-class work, it is not so much boys in general who talk more, but rather a small subset of boys (French and French 1984, Sunderland 1996). Nevertheless, the phenomenon undoubtedly exists, gendering both speaking practice opportunities and potential learning opportunities. In particular, a student who speaks to the teacher (either spontaneously, or having been invited to do so) is able to test a hypothesis about the workings of the target language. S/he can at the same time get affective as well as cognitive feedback, and make him or herself better known to the teacher (Stanworth 1983).

1.3 Topics and materials: there is potentially a greater range of both topics and materials than in most other subject classrooms

Though language teaching is often done against a background of a stipulated syllabus with a stipulated textbook that stipulates topics, in principle, language learning can be achieved through an unlimited range of topics. Accordingly, unique to language teaching is the possibility of any topic not only occurring in class but also being treated as relevant as carrier content for vocabulary, syntax, or language function, or for practice and development of reading, writing, speaking, listening, and translation skills. Indeed, the ideal role of the language classroom is arguably to extend the use of the target language to all possible topics. Constraints apart, this means that learners can be asked to read, write and talk about, and listen to anything. (The only other subject classroom of which this is true, arguably, is the mother tongue language classroom.)

Most teachers will, however, through choice or obligation, draw on a textbook. Many content analyses of gender in textbooks in the 1970s and 80s showed language textbooks to be gender-biased in a range of ways (e.g. Porecca 1984, Talansky 1986), as did linguistic analyses in the 1990s (e.g. Carroll and Kowitz 1994). Though this bias was not necessarily more than in other subject textbooks, it was particularly well-documented for language textbooks.

Gender bias in a textbook, however, cannot automatically be considered to disadvantage female learners, either in their learning or in the development of their gender identity. Textbooks in the classroom do not have a life of their own, but are mediated by the teacher (and the students). In language classrooms, however, the teacher can, in principle, move away from the topic provided and feel this is still pedagogically justifiable (Sunderland *et al* 1998). Since this movement may be in a progressive or sexist direction, teacher treatment of language textbooks may have a special potential to be gendered, or to gender classroom participants. Pedagogically, as regards language learning, this potentially wide-ranging use of the target language may augur well for girls if any L1 advantage (see 1.4) transfers to the FL classroom.

1.4. Attitudes and apparent ability: gender is more salient here than in many other subject classrooms

Different attitudes and abilities are characteristic of all curricular subjects and subject classrooms. In language education, however, attitudes to language learning tend to be markedly gendered. Students may not always express beliefs about languages being "girls' subjects" (Batters 1986); and in the Burstall *et al.* (1974) primary school study, there was no significant gender difference between girls' and boys' responses to "I am afraid to speak French". However in both Burstall's (1970) and Batters' studies, girls were overall more positive about language learning; as regards activities, girls and boys were equally positive only about speaking in Batters' study. In subject choice, in much of the world (the UK is perhaps an extreme example), girls opt for languages more than boys.

(Studies of adults' attitudes and motivations have, however, found few statistically significant gender differences [Muchnick and Wolfe 1992, Ludwig 1983, Bacon and Finnemann 1992].)

Some teachers tend to see girls as the better language learners, perhaps as having a "flair" for languages (itself a claim that may be made only for certain subjects), without necessarily feeling a need to seek an explanation for this, accepting it as "given". However, for many language teachers, gender is not particularly salient. Three studies are particularly relevant here. First, Powell and Batters (1986) found in a questionnaire study of language teachers that 42% disagreed with the statement "Neither boys nor girls think of languages in terms of masculine or feminine subjects", and only 30% agreed. Second, Burstall, in her 1970 study of Primary French, did not find that gender appeared in the teachers' reports in any significant way. Third, Aeginitou *et al* (1994), in an investigation of which gender issues concerned English teachers from a range of countries, suggested that gender was not very salient to most teachers at all.

Reasons for gendered attitudes are not clear-cut. Burstall *et al* (1974) found that boys were dissatisfied in language lessons because they wanted more speaking, and, interestingly, that girls in mixed-sex French classes were embarrassed by speaking and wanted to speak less. Gendered attitudes are, however, likely to be related to success (or lack of it). As regards performance, girls perform better in many foreign language examinations (e.g. Arnot *et al* 1996)[2], and teachers' view of girls as better language learners may not only result from an acceptance of stereotypes but from actual differences in performance in homework, tests, or exams. There may, of course, be a Pygmalion effect here. However, any test results must be partially a function of the test, and topics, tasks, and testers have all been found to be gendered in some way (Sunderland 1995a). Higher marks are thus not straightforward indicators of superior proficiency.

Like reasons for gendered attitudes, reasons for differences in performance are not clear. Beswick (1976) reported that

French teachers from 15 British schools believed that boys underachieved for three reasons: (a) they saw French as being less relevant to their career prospects than girls did, (b) girls' faster maturation helped them do the painstaking work necessary for language learning, and (c) there was "vocal inhibition in boys when attempting to make unfamiliar sounds in the presence of the girls". Powell and Batters (1986), in contrast, see boys' writing, not speaking, as causing them to fall behind.

Neither socially constructed factors, including attitudes, nor innate (sex) differences in ability can be ruled out as contributory explanations of gendered abilities in language learning (Burstall *et al.* 1974, Maccoby and Jacklin 1974). The same is true of those few differences in language learning styles and strategies which have been identified (Willing 1989, Oxford 1994). Maccoby and Jacklin claim that girls are innately superior to boys in some aspects of the L1, and, if true, this may spin off into the learning of a subsequent language, perhaps in terms of communicative ability generally, or simply confidence. Hirst (1982, p. 110), in a neurological investigation, concludes cautiously that "there may be sex differences in both linguistic ability and functional brain lateralisation, and the two may be causally connected". Ekstrand observes even more inconclusively that in the wider study of cognitive sex differences there are two clear tendencies: "inconsistency of findings" and "relative smallness of the differences" (1980, p. 203). His conclusion from his own investigation into innate sex differences in second language learning is that much evidence points in the direction of men and women being so alike that "almost all the behavioral variation may be explained by cultural factors" (1980, p. 251). And Klann-Delius concludes that "possible sex differences in the structure or the rate of language acquisition...cannot be made plausible by biological hypotheses" (1981, p. 13).

Some or even all gender differences in language learning ability and use of the first and subsequent languages are then likely to reflect socially constructed gender differences. (This would shed some explanatory light in particular on the fact that in all-boys' schools, foreign languages are much more popular than in mixed-sex schools (Loulidi 1990).) What must be remembered, of course, is that, whatever their origin, any gender "differences", in style, strategy, ability, or performance, represent tendencies that are not by any means fixed, and that there are not only overlaps between male and female learners but also many similarities.

1.5 Language learners' identity

Relationships between language and identity are complex, as studies of language, ethnicity, and bilingualism have shown. I will simply restate here Ivanic's (1998, p. 12) observation that identity from a social constructionist point of view is "the result of affiliation to particular beliefs and possibilities which are available in... [a] social context." To the extent, then, that the language classroom may make available new beliefs and possibilities, so that one may even feel like a different person when speaking the target language, the language classroom has the special potential to challenge or add to a learner's identity, or even create an additional identity for the learner, as well as to enhance or make poorer his or her self-image.[3] As regards gender, the "boundaries" of femininity may be more fluid than those of masculinity (Chodorow 1978, Sunderland 1995b, Phillips 1994), since in some ways there are now fewer limits on girls' and women's behavior than on those of boys and men. Thus, though girls may be embarrassed to speak in front of boys (Burstall *et al.* 1974), female learners may also in principle be more open to some of the possible changes in (self-) image and identity that speaking a foreign language (including the "not-myself" verbal behavior of dialogues and role plays) can bring.

2. What are the implications of these five characteristic areas of the language classroom for language classroom research in general, and for research into gender and the language classroom in particular?

By classroom research, I mean research centered on the classroom, i.e. research which in whole or in part relies on data collected from the classroom (see also Allwright 1988, van Lier 1988, Nunan 1991). Studies of textbooks alone would thus not constitute classroom research, whereas studies of student use of the textbook in the classroom would. In this section I look at some of the research questions (RQs) suggested by the discussion in the preceding pages. In Section 3, I will move on to language classroom research issues in general and as pertaining to gender. The first two areas ~ language use (1.1) and the role of the teacher and distribution of talking time (1.2) ~ suggest RQs which are particularly relevant to the language classroom, with the aim of describing and understanding it. The third area ~ topics and materials (1.3) ~ points to unanswered RQs. The fourth area ~ attitudes and ability (1.4) ~ though important, is arguably less immediately amenable to classroom research and is traditionally researched outside it. The fifth area ~ identity (1.5) ~ has indeed been researched in classrooms, e.g. in bilingual settings (e.g. Martin-Jones and Saxena 1995), but this would have to be the subject of another paper.

It is important to attempt to identify what these RQs might be, as part of a wider project to find out whether the language classroom is a "special case". For example, because of their alleged "flair" for languages, are girls dominated by boys in language classrooms as much as it has been suggested they are in other classrooms? The first three areas, I argue, are all underexplored by classroom research. (This is in interesting contrast to the many studies on attitudes, abilities, and perceptions of language classroom participants, and of foreign language textbooks *qua* textbooks).

Some of the RQs identified below have been asked; others, to my knowledge, have not, but very fruitfully could be. I will take areas (1.1) and (1.2) together, then look at the third (1.3):

<u>Language use (1.1)</u> and <u>the role of the teacher and distribution of talking time (1.2)</u>. Research questions can be asked about (a) the language used by the teacher to the students in whole-class work, (b) the (related) language used by the students to the teacher in whole-class work, and (c) the language used by the students to each other in pairwork or groupwork. Given that, in most language classrooms, both the target language and the learners' mother tongue (or at least one of the latter) is used, RQs in each of these areas can have language as a variable. Hitherto, however, much of the emphasis in gender and language classroom research has made little if any distinction between target and first language use

(e.g. Gass and Varonis 1986, Provo 1991, Pica 1992). This gap could benefit from being filled. My own study (Sunderland 1996) aimed at doing precisely this, but was a study of only one classroom, i.e. a very specific context of a German as a FL classroom (with children aged 11-12) in a British comprehensive school. My intention here is to promote other, similar studies in different language learning contexts.

Given, then, that RQs can be asked of both the target language (TL) and the L1, in the three areas identified above, we have the following possible areas of research, with some examples (only) of specific topics:

Target Language and L1(s)		
(TL or L1) (a) Language of teacher to students	I.	Amount of talk directed to females/males (*number of words/turns*)
	II.	Type of feedback given to females/males
(TL or L1) (b) Language of students to teacher	I.	Number of times females/males volunteered an answer to a teacher's question
	II.	Types of question addressed to teacher by females/males
(TL or L1) (c) Language of students to each other	I.	Presence or absence of prompts/encouragement/backchannelling by females/males to females/males
	II.	Syntax of suggestions by females/males to the group

There are gaps, I suggest, in many of these topic areas (see below). There are other gaps too. Much of the emphasis in gender and language classroom research has been quantitative. With the increasing acceptability of qualitative research, this appears to be changing. It is beyond the scope of this paper to discuss entirely qualitative approaches to research into gender and classrooms (but see Davies 1989, Jones 1993, Lewis and Simon 1986, for a qualitative study of gender identity in the classroom, see Sunderland 1995). However, I hope to go down the qualitative road by showing how quantitative approaches can become much more meaningful through the study of "types" of a given feature X, as well as of feature X's frequency of occurrence.

Other gaps include age (most work on gender in language classrooms has been with adults), language classes taught by teachers who share an L1 with the students, classes in which the language being taught is not English, and whole class work.

(Perhaps because pair- and groupwork is characteristic of language classrooms, more studies of gender and language classroom talk have in fact been done on groupwork than whole classwork, e.g. Gass and Varonis 1986, Provo 1991, Holmes 1994; see Yepez [1994] for an exception.)

In what follows I will suggest ways in which the "whole class" gap can be addressed in conjunction with the "two languages" gap. Let us consider those aspects of gendered classroom talk which can be investigated, and then look at those that have been investigated, inside or outside the language classroom, to date. Starting with the widely-acknowledged IRF (initiation-response-feedback) pattern (Bellack *et al.* 1966, Sinclair and Coulthard 1975), we can look at the language of: **(a) teacher initiation, (b) student responses, (c) teacher feedback to student responses.** However, not all that happens in a classroom, even in whole-class work, fits neatly into this pattern. There are also: **(a) student initiations (to the teacher), (b) teacher responses, (c) student feedback to teacher responses.**

The last three utterance types are not how the IRF pattern is usually interpreted, though there is no reason why it should not be. It is important to remember (and this can be demonstrated empirically, e.g. Sunderland 1996) that students do sometimes give some form of feedback to (though may not actually evaluate) teachers' responses to their (the students') questions.

We can add "teacher comments" and "student comments" to this list – a "comment" being definable as an utterance which is not an initiation, a response, or feedback to a response. A teacher comment such as "Harry's back today" may be important in that it allows Harry to know he has been noticed; absence of comment may suggest he has not been. Alternatively, it can make a student feel s/he has been unfairly singled out. Student comments may indicate confidence and the willingness of a student to be spontaneous, and (by definition) to speak even when not spoken to. This spontaneity could create a learning opportunity, disrupt others' learning, and/or do something else entirely.

There are thus at least eight discourse areas in relation to "whole class talk" about which specific, operationalisable RQs could be asked. Relevant, at least potentially, to all subject classrooms, few have been investigated in the context of the language classroom, even fewer specifically in relation to gender in the language classroom. In the course of my own study I found that none had been investigated in terms of gender and specifically differentiated use of the target language and the L1.

The table below indicates which of the eight classroom utterance types identified have to my knowledge been looked at in relation to gender, and whether prior to my study they had been looked at in relation to the language classroom. The second column does not aim to be comprehensive. (The table does not include my own study, for example, which looked at all of these areas.)

	Looked at before in relation to gender?	Looked at before in relation to gender and the language classroom?
Teacher solicits	Kelly 1988, Dart and Clarke 1988, Serbin *et al.* 1973, Good, Sykes, and Brophy 1973, Leinhard *et al.* 1979	Yepez 1994
Student responses	Dart and Clarke 1988	N
Teacher feedback	Good, Sykes, and Brophy 1973	Yepez 1994
Student solicits	Dart and Clarke 1988, Whyte 1984	N
Teacher responses	Kelly 1988 (?)	Yepez 1994 (?)
Student feedback	N	N
Students comments	N	N
Teacher comments	Kelly 1988 (?)	Yepez 1994 (?)

As indicated, since there is the potential for any utterance to be in either the L1 or mother tongue, language could be a variable in any research question. One example of a research question might be: *What is the proportion of male and female students who volunteered unsolicited answers to the teacher's questions in:* (1) **The mother tongue?** (2) **The target language?**

These gaps in gender and language classroom research – in particular, on student talk in whole-class work – indicate there is plenty of scope for fresh research into gender and talk in the language classroom. I would argue that this scope should be capitalised on, as such studies may pay interesting dividends. *(I will indicate some of my own results at the end of this paper.)*

Topic and materials (1.3): As already indicated, there exists a large body of research into gender bias in language teaching materials (e.g. Porecca 1984, Talansky 1986, Hellinger 1980). Content and linguistic analyses have indicated gender bias to be rife in the form of female invisibility, gender stereotyping, and even degradation of women. There is, however, some evidence (e.g. Jones *et al.* 1997) that the situation is improving.

These studies, being text-based, cannot be said to constitute classroom research. This, I suggest, represents their limitation. As far as any influence of textbooks on language learning and gender identity is concerned, much will depend on the response of the reader him- or herself. In the classroom, this response may be mediated by the use made of the textbook by the teacher and students. For example, faced with a gender-biased text, the teacher's options include endorsing it, ignoring the features of bias, or subverting it in some way. Correspondingly, faced with a "progressive" text, a teacher has similar choices. What is done with a text primarily requires classroom, not textual research. Little such research, however, has been done, in the language or indeed any other subject classroom (but see Abraham 1989, Stodolsky 1989, Bonkowski 1995, Hutchinson 1996, and Sunderland *et al.* 2000b, on doing such research in the language classroom). Research questions might cover not only how a given teacher uses a given text, but also wider questions, such as:

(a) **Given a "progressive" text, how do teachers tend to treat it?**

(b) **Given a gender-biased text, how do teachers tend to treat it?**

(c) **If they themselves are concerned about gender bias, are teachers more likely to:**
   (1) contest bias where they identify it?
   (2) do full justice to a progressive text?

(d) **Which is more widespread** (and hence more of a problem, with implications for writers, publishers and teacher educators), **teachers not doing justice to the progressive aspect of a progressive text, or teachers endorsing gender-biased texts?**

(e) **What is the role of student contributions to the above?**

My own early research in this area with colleagues (Sunderland *et al.* 1998) indicates a worrying tendency for teachers to simply ignore "progressive" features of textbook texts. It would seem important to know if this pattern is a widespread one.

3. Gender issues and classroom research; *classroom research issues and gender*

In this final section I will look at wider issues relevant to gender research in the language classroom. In particular, these are (3.1) the issue of two languages; (3.2) the selection of a research site, access, and acceptance; (3.3) researching group- and pairwork; (3.4) transcription issues; (3.5) research ethics; and (3.6) publication issues.

3.1. The issue of two languages

Much research has been done by native speakers of English in classes learning English. I have suggested that one gap in the literature is classrooms in which the target language is not English. This may raise issues for the Anglophone researcher. In particular, she or he may not be proficient in the language being taught. Though it may seem foolish for a teacher to do research in such a classroom, there may be compelling reasons to do so. It may be the only one in which the teacher is willing to be observed, or there may be good reasons not to use others.

What are the implications for the research if the researcher is not proficient in the language being taught? He or she may then not fully understand what is going on in the class itself – though this will depend on the level of the class, the degree to which the language is contextualised, use of the L1 (if this is also the researcher's L1), and his/her own level of proficiency in the target language. Secondly, if the lessons are being audiotaped and transcribed, there will be transcription problems (though these can be overcome to an extent with the help of dictionaries and, ideally, help with the transcripts from a native-speaker or good user of the target language). Thirdly, and more seriously, when doing the data analysis, lack of familiarity with the target language may make it impossible for the researcher to work out what is going on, and accordingly, impossible to encode or classify a given utterance (in any case often a problematic task, since the tape conveys few contextual features). At what point, for example, in a question-answer session, does the teacher move from expanding on one student's answer to asking the next question, assuming both of these are done in the target language? This can only be (partially) resolved by consulting a speaker of the language (ideally, the teacher herself).

However, I would like to suggest, oddly enough, that lack of familiarity with the target language may *in some ways* be an advantage. A researcher who is familiar with the language being taught may find him- or herself concentrating on the language at the expense of observing or taking fieldnotes. Though this brought its own problems, in my own study I found that not knowing German meant I was able to let the language "wash over" me, in contrast to a French class I also observed, in which I frequently found myself "testing" my linguistic ability – not what I was there to do at all.

3.2 Selection of a research site, access, and acceptance

• *SELECTION:* As indicated, two gaps in the literature are studies of non-English classes, and language classes taught by a teacher who shares the students' L1. There is, of course, no shortage of such language classes worldwide, and selection of one such could result in interesting findings.

Teachers are rarely enthusiastic about being observed. A language teacher may feel that any lack of command of the subject matter (the target language) is particularly evident in the language classroom (I have already mentioned the possibility that one or more students may have a superior target language command), and perhaps traceable through the teaching strategies the teacher adopts (Wright 1992). If so, he or she may be understandably reluctant to allow a researcher into his or her class. However, important in any classroom research is working with a teacher who is willing, even interested in having the researcher in her classroom. A willing teacher can make all the difference to a piece of research (as can an unwilling one, in the opposite direction).

For the researcher working in mixed-sex language classrooms, very important, I would suggest, is having at least an approximately equal number of female and male students; otherwise what might seem like a "gender effect" may in fact be a "minority" or "majority" group effect.

• *ACCESS:* Many gender researchers are women (though with the advent of work on masculinity the proportion may be getting less). Does this make it easier or harder to get access to a language classroom? Milroy (1980) notes that as a woman walking around Belfast to collect her data on language variation, she was potentially less threatening to the community and thus safer than a male researcher would have been. Issues of access are rarely so dramatic in classroom research but may still be present. Writers on "being a female researcher" have identified both advantages and disadvantages (e.g. Easterday *et al.* 1982). Like Milroy, a female researcher may be less threatening to an establishment than a male, which may facilitate her access. On the other hand, if she is, correspondingly, taken less seriously than a male would be, working in a school where research has prestige, being female may actually hinder her.

• *ACCEPTANCE:* Once in the language classroom, since the language teaching profession in many countries is a relatively "feminine" one (Powell 1986), a female researcher may be less conspicuous than a male would be, and less conspicuous than she would in a mixed-sex "masculine" subject classroom such as physics. Acceptance by the learners may be of particular value both in obtaining naturalistic data, and in participant interviews with students and teachers.[4]

Women researching gender are often seen as motivated by feminist concerns. Experience suggests this perception to be broadly correct. In her research into gender and classroom interaction, the feminist researcher may expect to find some manifestation of female disadvantage. (She may even want to find it, believing that exposure will help bring about change, such as single-sex classes in mixed-sex schools.) Others may hope their data will show that, for once, girls are coping well, even very well. Whatever her motivation, the feminist researcher working on gender may be perceived as biased, compared with women working in other areas (or, indeed, with men working on gender). However, the feminist researcher is likely to be particularly aware of her sympathies and concerns and will thus be able to acknowledge and "monitor" them in a way that a less "committed" researcher may not.

Most readers of this volume will probably share the view that no-one is "gender-neutral". I hope that most readers also view this subjectivity as a potential advantage. The female researcher who shares a similar consciousness of the issues in question with female teachers (i.e. most language teachers) may produce a sharper, more meaningful, and more coherent interview and interpretation of it. However, as in any other context, single-sex interview talk may be different from mixed-sex interview talk (e.g. West and Zimmerman 1983), and this phenomenon is likely to have an impact on any interviewing that is carried out.

3.3 Researching group- and pairwork

If pair- and groupwork are characteristic of the language classroom, then they need to be researched, as indeed they have been (Holmes 1994, Gass and Varonis 1986) especially if, as has been demonstrated in one context (Holmes 1994), male students tend to dominate in mixed-sex pair- and groupwork. Recording pair- and groupwork in naturalistic classrooms is, however, notoriously difficult (for the simple reason that talk from the adjacent pair/group is picked up when one group is being recorded), often resulting in little more than fragments of recorded data. The researcher in the naturalistic classroom who wishes to investigate on-task (and/or off-task) student to student talk may need to compromise her principles, and either work in very small (adult?) classes, or else work with a group who, for the purposes of the study, are temporarily working physically outside the main classroom.

3.4 Transcription issues

Transcription of classroom data is of concern to all classroom researchers who choose to "preserve real time" by audiorecording lessons. All transcription must be selective (van Lier 1988, p. 80). What is included will depend on the purpose of the study, i.e. the transcription system adopted should be one which will enable the researcher to answer the research questions, and should be no more complex than that.

Transcribing language lessons involves certain decisions common to the transcription of any spoken data, e.g. whether and how to indicate pauses, whether and how to indicate overlapping speech. However, issues specific to the transcription of on-task or off-task talk in a language lesson soon arise (issues shared by research in bilingual and multilingual classrooms). Typically, two (or more) languages will be spoken; both will need to be transcribed. The researcher will almost certainly want to distinguish between the two languages, using, say, italics for one and a standard or other contrasting font for the other, to facilitate both analysis and readability. Transcribing two languages means occasionally using letters which do not exist in English, such as the German letter ß, or even, for some studies, using two completely different scripts (e.g. if English is the mother tongue and Chinese the target language a different font may not be necessary). One or more of the languages may also need to be translated (see Altani 1993).

Yet another set of decisions has to be made concerning transcription of spelling in the target language, including of spelling games such as "Hangman". To aid readability, the researcher may decide not to write each letter phonetically, but may simply decide to give the actual letter, perhaps capitalised to avoid confusion. This will again mean sometimes using language-specific letters like the German ß. A special problem concerns spelling games which use students' names, something that is probably only done in the language classroom. Whereas spelling the name out accurately clearly destroys anonymity, spelling out a fictional name may render this part of the transcript incomprehensible.[5]

There are also gender-related transcription issues to contend with. Whether emphasis is on gender tendencies, or the discursive construction of gender, the identification of speaker sex must be crucial. S1, S2, etc. is not sufficient! To make analysis possible and findings reliable and valid, male and female students must be distinguishable, at least most of the time. Depending on the study, it may be sufficient to indicate "B" for each boy and "G" for each girl; if the researcher is also concerned to study diversity and hence individuals, labels like G1, G2, or (preferably) actual, fictionalised names are necessary. As with any subject classroom, responses to teacher's questions can be attributed to an individual if the teacher names the student first; likewise, questions to the teacher if the teacher uses the questioner's name in the response are similarly attributable. Harder are unsolicited student comments, especially if these are ignored by the teacher, as are student responses solicited by gaze, gesture, or words such as "you", and voices in pair- and groupwork. Not only do students' words (naturally) overlap; in the case of younger boys whose voices have not yet broken, it may be almost impossible to distinguish them from girls in the group.[6]

3.5 Ethics

Classroom participants do not simply help the researcher by tolerating her presence, discussing their perceptions, and filling in the gaps in her transcripts, they also enable her to earn her Ph.D., leaving the researcher with what Labov (1982) referred to as a "debt incurred". A version of the dissertation can be left with the school; the students can perhaps be made aware of the findings through the creation of a special information gap or transfer exercise, discussion topic, reading or listening comprehension (Dick Allwright, personal communication). This would be much harder to do in other subject classrooms, where the range of acceptable topics is much narrower. It is, however, the teacher who tends actively *to put herself out to* help the researcher, and to whom the greatest debt of gratitude is owed. In the Anglo-American discourse of the 1970s, this would have been considered "unsisterly" (it is not the teacher who gets her Ph.D. out of the experience). She may, of course, wish to become a co-author herself, but, if not, is likely to welcome copies of resultant publications. At the very least, s/he needs full acknowledgement in such publications.

3.6 Publication issues

Recently, the emphasis in gender research has been on similarities as well as differences, and on how classroom discourse constructs (rather than reveals or reflects) gender. However the danger remains that "exposed" gender "differences" make for more sensational reading – and may, still, be of more interest to journals and professional publications – than similarities. Gender differences can be and often are mis-re-represented by those conservatives who celebrate gender differences, using not a "disadvantage" discourse but an essentialist, *vive la différence* one (Cameron 1993, Sunderland 1996). Gender similarities may not be "marked", but for precisely this reason need to be continuously and consistently documented. I would also argue that findings which represent female students as something other than "victims" of male dominance should likewise be highlighted.

CONCLUSION

The mixed-sex language classroom is, I would claim, an important and rather special epistemological site for gender research. Put simply, because language is a curricular subject in which girls and women tend to perform well, it is interesting to consider (a) the effect and (b) the manifestations of male dominance – if male dominance there is. Given male dominance and higher female grades, there is not, however, logically, a contradiction – it may be that girls and women would do even better if the male dominance did not occur.

In my own (1996) study of a German classroom in a British comprehensive school, in which I looked at differential teacher treatment by gender, and gender differences in student talk, the boys received more teacher attention than the girls in a variety of areas. However, there were also many areas of similarity, and many differences which were not statistically significant (see also Sunderland 1998). In particular:

(1) The distribution of different types of teacher feedback to "broadly correct" and "broadly incorrect" answers did not vary with gender.

(2) *Neither* boys *nor* girls were more likely to have their academic or non-academic "initiations" ignored by the teacher.

There were also some interesting statistically significant or nearly significant gender tendencies in *quality* of talk:

(1) Compared with boys, the teacher asked the girls a greater proportion of academic solicits to which they were expected to respond in German *(approaching significance at 5% level)*.

(2) Compared with boys, the teacher asked the girls a greater proportion of questions which required an answer of more than one word *(significant at 5% level)*.

(3) The girls asked longer questions of the teacher than did the boys *(significant at 5% level)*.

(4) The girls volunteered more words and answers in German than did the boys *(significant at 5% level)*.

These interesting and in many ways unpredictable findings, I suggest, indicate a form of "academic femininity" operating in this language classroom. Such findings may be unique to this classroom. In particular, they may be an effect of the fact that the students in question were eleven and twelve years old, i.e. just out of primary school, not having embarked on the explorations of new gender relations and identities characteristic of adolescence. However, they also illustrate the value of both (a) investigating gender in whole-class language classroom talk (these girls were clearly not victims) and (b) investigating differential mother tongue/target language use in studies of gender in the language classroom – which, as I hope I have shown, can be done.

ENDNOTES

1. The many other contributing factors include school factors – level, funding, intake; student factors – age, sex, perceived ability, family background; teacher factors – training, beliefs about learning; geographical factors – cultural context, beliefs about education.

2. The fact that girls seem to get both better results than boys, and less teacher attention, is sometimes identified as a paradox. Logically, of course, given more attention, they might get even better results. Alternatively, it may be unreasonable to expect a relationship between teacher attention and exam results.

3. Self-esteem may be gendered; certainly attributions of success and failure appear to be (e.g. Licht and Dweck 1987, Ryckman and Peckham 1987). And as self-esteem may be related to task performance (Heyde-Parsons 1983), boys' and girls' self-esteem could vary with performance on, say, written exercises, multiple choice questions, vocabulary memorization, and dialogue design and performance.

4. I found that most of the children in the class I was observing who spontaneously made contact with me were girls – though I suspect this was a "same-sex" rather than a "female researcher" phenomenon.

5. The transcriber of the language lesson will also have to decide whether and how to indicate linguistic errors. As regards pronunciation errors, s/he will probably ignore them and continue to use standard orthographic spelling; if s/he is not focusing on pronunciation, this does not represent too much of a compromise of validity. However, any subsequent teacher correction will then, as the transcription stands, not make sense, so some indication that there has been an error, such as underlining, may be used instead. Teacher correction of errors at a word and syntactic level will make sense to a user of the target language, but a non-user who is not analysing the transcript will have to take this on trust. (A researcher who is a non-user of the language would be well-advised to choose a focus other than errors.)

6. One solution is to "employ" one of the learners in the class to listen to the recordings, and identify the voices (as well as, possibly, some of the more unclear utterances).

ABOUT THE AUTHOR

Jane Sunderland is a Lecturer in the Department of Linguistics and Modern Language, Lancaster University, UK, where she teaches "Gender and Language", "Language and Education", and "Language and Identity" courses. She is also Co-ordinator of the Ph.D. in Applied Linguistics by Thesis and Coursework Program (an unusual program for the UK). Her research interests are gender outside as well as inside the classroom, student questions and student follow-up to teachers' responses to those questions, and the use and value of e-mail on distance learning programs.

BIBLIOGRAPHY

Abraham, J. (1989). "Teacher ideology and sex roles in curriculum texts". British Journal of Sociology of Education 10/1: 33 – 51.

Aeginitou, V. et al. (1994). "Investigating teachers' concerns about gender issues in the English language classroom". CRILE Working Paper 19, Department of Linguistics and Modern English Language, Lancaster University.

Allwright, R.L. (1988). Observation in the Language Classroom. London: Longman.

Altani, C. (1993). "Presentation of Greek data to Anglophone readers: transcription and translation issues". In Gimenez, T. and Sunderland, J. (eds.). Research Processes in Applied Linguistics, Dept. of Linguistics and Modern English Language, Lancaster University, UK.

Arnot, M., M. David and G. Weiner (1996). Educational Reforms and Gender Equality in Schools. Equal Opportunities Commission Research Discussion Series No. 17. Manchester: EOC.

Bacon, S. and M. Finnemann (1992). "Sex differences in self-reported beliefs about foreign-language learning and authentic oral and written input". Language Learning 42/4: 471 - 95.

Batters, J. (1986). "Do boys really think languages are just girl-talk?" Modern Languages 67/2: 75 - 79.

Bellack, A. et al. (1966). The Language of the Classroom. New York: Teachers' College Press.

Beswick, C. (1976). "Mixed or single-sex for French?" Audio-Visual Language Journal, 34 - 38.

Bonkowski, F. (1995). Teacher Use and Interpretation of Textbook Materials in the Secondary ESL Classroom in Quebec. Ph.D. thesis, Lancaster University.

Burstall, C. (1970). French in the Primary School. Slough: NFER.

Burstall, C., M. Jamieson, S. Cohen and M. Hargreaves (1974). Primary French in the Balance. Slough: NFER.

Cameron, D. (1993). "Rethinking language and gender studies". Plenary paper, 10th AILA Congress, Amsterdam.

Carroll, D. and J. Kowitz (1994). "Using concordancing techniques to study gender stereotyping in ELT textbooks". In J. Sunderland (ed.) Exploring Gender: Questions and Implications for English Language Education. Hemel Hempstead: Prentice Hall.

Chodorow, N. (1978). The Reproduction of Mothering. Berkeley, CA: University of California Press.

Clark, A. and J. Trafford (1995). "Boys into modern languages: an investigation in attitudes and performance between boys and girls in modern languages". Gender and Education 7/3: 315 - 325.

Dart, B. and J. Clarke (1988). "Sexism in schools: a new look". Educational Review 40/1: 41 - 9.

Davies, B. (1989). Frogs and Snails and Feminist Tales: Pre-school Children and Gender. Sydney: Allen and Unwin.

Easterday, L. et al. (1982). "The making of a female researcher: role problems in fieldwork". In R. Burgess (ed.) Field Research: a Sourcebook and Field Manual. London: Allen and Unwin.

Ekstrand, L. (1980). "Sex differences in second language learning?: empirical studies and a discussion of related findings". International Review of Applied Psychology 29: 205 - 259.

French, J. and P. French (1984). "Gender imbalances in the primary classroom: an interactional account.". Educational Research 26/2: 127 - 136.

Gass, S. and E. Varonis (1986). "Sex differences in nonnative speaker-nonnative speaker interactions." In R. Day (ed.) Talking to Learn: Conversation in Second Language Acquisition. New York: Newbury House.

Gilbert, J. (1992). "Achieving equity in small-group discussions". Working Papers on Language, Gender and Sexism 2/2: 55 -73.

Good, T, N. Sykes and J. Brophy (1973). "Effects of teacher sex and student sex on classroom interaction". Journal of Educational Psychology 65: 74- 87.

Hellinger, M. (1981). "For men must work and women must weep: sexism in English language textbooks used in German schools". In C. Kramarae (ed.) The Voices and Words of Women and Men. New York: Pergamon.

Heyde-Parsons, A.W. (1983). "Self-esteem and the acquisition of French". In K. Bailey et al. (eds.) Studies in Second Language Acquisition: Series on Issues in Second Language Research. Rowley, MA: Newbury House.

Hirst, (1982). "An evaluation of evidence for innate sex differences in linguistic ability". Journal of Psycholinguistic Research 11/2: 95 – 113.

Hollway, W. (1984). "Gender differences and the production of the subject". In J. Henriques et al. (eds.) Changing the Subject. London: Methuen.

Holmes, J. (1994). "Improving the lot of female language learners". In J. Sunderland (ed.) Exploring Gender: Questions and Implications for English Language Education. Hemel Hempstead: Prentice Hall.

Hutchinson, E. (1996). What Do Teachers and Learners Actually Do with Textbooks?: Teacher and Learner Use of a Fisheries-based ELT Textbook in the Philippines. Ph.D. dissertation, Lancaster University, UK.

Ivanic, R. (1998). Writing and Identity. Amsterdam: John Benjamins.

Jenkins, N. and J. Cheshire (1990). "Gender issues in the GCSE oral English examination: Part 1". Language and Education 4/4: 261 – 292.

Jones, A. (1993). "Becoming a 'Girl': post-structuralist suggestions for educational research". Gender and Education 5/2: 157 – 166.

Jones, M., C. Kitetu and J. Sunderland (1997). "Discourse roles, gender and language textbook dialogues: who learns what from John and Sally?" Gender and Education 9/4: 469 – 490.

Kelly, A. (1988). "Gender differences in teacher-pupil interactions: a meta-analytic review". Research in Education 39: 1 – 23.

Klann-Delius, G. (1881). "Sex and language acquisition: is there any influence?" Journal of Pragmatics 5: 1-25.

Knubb-Manninen, G. (1988). "Cultural background and second language acquisition". Scandinavian Journal of Education 32/2: 93 – 100.

Labov, W. 1982. "Objectivity and commitment in linguistic science: the case of the Black English trial in Ann Arbor". Language in Society 11: 165 – 201.

Leder, G. 1987. "Teacher student interaction: a case study". Education Studies in Mathematics 18: 255 – 271.

Leinhardt, S. et al. (1979). "Learning what's taught: sex differences in instruction". Journal of Educational Psychology 71/4: 432-9.

Lewis, M. and R. Simon (1986). "A discourse not intended for her: learning and teaching within patriarchy". Harvard Educational Review 56: 457 – 472.

Licht, B. and C. Dweck (1987). 'Sex differences in achievement orientations'. In M. Arnot and G. Weiner (eds.) Gender and the Politics of Schooling. London: Unwin Hyman.

Loulidi, R. (1990). "Is language learning really a female business?" Language Learning Journal 1: 40 – 43.

Ludwig, J. (1983). "Attitudes and expectations: a profile of female and male students of college French, German and Spanish". The Modern Language Journal 67/3: 216 - 27.

Maccoby, E. and C. Jacklin (1974). The Psychology of Sex Differences. Stanford, CA: Stanford U.P.

Martin-Jones, M. and M. Saxena (1995). "Turn-taking, power asymmetries and the positioning of bilingual participants in classroom discourse". Centre for Language in Social Life Working Paper 65. Dept. of Linguistics and Modern English Language, Lancaster University.

Merrett, F. and K. Wheldall (1992). "Teachers' use of praise and reprimands to boys and girls". Education Review 44/1: 73 - 9.

Milroy, L. (1980). Language and Social Networks. Oxford: Basil Blackwell.

Muchnick, A. and D. Wolfe (1992). "Attitudes and motivations of American students of Spanish". The Canadian Modern Language Review 38: 274 - 76.

Nunan, D. (1991). "Methods in second language classroom-oriented research". Studies in Second Language Acquisition 13: 249 – 274.

Oakley, A. (1981). "Interviewing women: a contradiction in terms". In H. Roberts (ed.) Doing Feminist Research. London: Routledge and Kegan Paul.

Oxford, R. (1994). "La différence continue....: gender differences' in second/foreign language learning styles and strategies". In J. Sunderland (ed.) Exploring Gender: Questions and Implications for English Language Education. Hemel Hempstead: Prentice Hall.

Peck, Antony (1988). Language Teachers at Work: a Description of Methods. Hemel Hempstead: Prentice Hall.

Phillips, A. (1994). The Trouble with Boys. London: Pandora.

Pica, T. et al.(1992). "Language learning through interaction: what role does gender play?" Studies in Second Language Acquisition 13: 343 - 76.

Porecca, K. (1984). "Sexism in current ESL textbooks". TESOL Quarterly 18/4: 705 - 23.

Powell, R. (1986). Boys, Girls and Languages in School. London: Centre for Information on Language Teaching and Research (CILT).

Powell, R. and J. Batters (1986). "Sex of teacher and the image of foreign languages in schools". Educational Studies 12/3: 245 - 54.

Provo, J. (1991). "Sex differences in nonnative speaker interaction". The Language Teacher XV/7: 25 - 28.

Ryckman, D. and P. Peckham (1987). "Gender differences in attributions for success and failure situations across subject areas". Journal of Educational Research 81/2: 120 - 125.

Sadker, M. and D. Sadker (1985). "Sexism in the schoolroom of the '80s". Psychology Today, March: 54 - 57.

Serbin, L. (1973). "A comparison of teacher response to the preacademic and problem behaviour of boys and girls". Child Development 44: 796 - 804.

Sinclair, J.M. and R.M. Coulthard (1975). Towards an Analysis of Discourse: the English Used by Teachers and Pupils. Oxford: OUP.

Stanworth, M. (1983). Gender and Schooling. London: Hutchinson.

Stodolsky, S. (1989). "Is teaching really by the book?" In Jackson, P. and S. Haroountian-Gordon (eds.) From Socrates to Software: the Teacher as Text and the Text as Teacher. The National Society for the Study of Education (USA): 159 – 184.

Sunderland, J. (1995a). "Gender and language testing". Language Testing Update 17: 24 - 35.

———— (1995b). "'We're boys, miss!': finding gendered identities and looking for gendering of identities in the foreign language classroom". In S. Mills (ed.) Language and Gender: Interdisciplinary Perspectives. Harlow: Longman.

———— (1996). "Gendered Discourse in the Foreign Language Classroom: Teacher-Student and Student-Teacher Talk, and the Social Construction of Children's Femininities and Masculinities". Ph.D. thesis, Lancaster University.

———— (1998). "Girls being quiet: a problem for foreign language classrooms?" Language Teaching Research 2/1: 48 – 82.

———— (2000a). "Review Article: Issues of Gender and Language in Second and Foreign Language Education." Language Teaching. 33/4: 203 - 223.

———— (2000b). "From Gender Bias in the Text to the Teacher Talk around the Text". (With Fauziah Abdul Rahim, Maire Cowley, Christina Leontzakou & Julie Shattuck). Linguistics & Education 11/2: 1–36.

Swann, J. and D. Graddol (1988). "Gender inequalities in classroom talk". English in Education 22/1: 48 - 65.

Talansky, S. (1986). "Sex role stereotyping in TEFL teaching materials". Perspectives XI/3: 32 - 41.

Van Lier, L. (1988). The Classroom and the Language Learner: Ethnography and Second-Language Classroom Research. London: Longman.

West, C. and D. Zimmerman (1983). "Small insults: a study of interruptions in cross-sex conversations between unacquainted persons". In Thorne, B. et al. (eds.) Language, Gender and Society. Rowley, Mass.: Newbury House.

Whyte, (1984). "Observing sex-stereotypes and interactions in the school lab and workshop". Educational Review 36/1: 75 - 86.

Wilkinson, L.C. and C. Marrett (eds., 1985). Gender Influences in Classroom Interaction. New York: Academic Press.

Willing, K. (1989). Learning Styles in Adult Migrant Education. Adelaide: National Curriculum Research Council.

Yepez, M. (1994). "An observation of gender-specific teacher behavior in the ESL classroom". Sex Roles 30, 1/2: 121 - 133.

SEXIST LANGUAGE
AND
INSTRUCTION IN WRITING

by
Michael Newman
Queens College - CUNY

ABSTRACT

This chapter describes an approach that writing teachers can adopt to promote gender fairness in student writing. This approach focuses on meaning rather than decontextualized usage rules. "Correcting" students' forms that may be seen as biased only serves to take away the authority from the person who should be the author without getting at the real issues involved. Instead, it is suggested that teachers point out any unintentional and hidden meanings that students may be expressing through their usages.

FEMINIST CRITIQUE AS PRESCRIPTION

Although it is not normally described as such, feminist language critique is a form of prescription. In other words, it is an effort to influence language -- specifically, to discourage certain forms of expression and promote others. It is important to recognize this prescriptive nature, not to disqualify feminist critique, but to understand its problems and possibilities. After all, while prescription is unfashionable today among language scholars, it is an activist tradition of thought concerning language. This tradition is at once ancient, dating back to the Indian grammarians of the Fifth Century B.C.E. (Smith 1983), deeply ideological in nature (Crowley 1989), and undiminished in its influence on speakers.

The one defining characteristic of prescription in language is an apparent focus on manner rather than content of expression. Here lies its central problem. Take, for example, the following imaginary statement about a female college student by a male classmate: *Tracy's the kind of girl who's really going places.*

We need not be upset by what this young man, let's call him Matt, wished to say to complain that his statement is sexist. All we need to do is point out that there is something wrong with his referring to an adult his own age as a girl. It is unlikely, after all, that he would refer to a male classmate as a boy. Our criticism may then be based on the probably unintentional connotations of his unequal usage of these two terms. Even in carefully planned writing the same issue can arise. Imagine that Matt writes the following sentence in a research report:

> Man is endangering the species' survival
> by his lack of environmental awareness.

There is nothing *overtly* misogynist here. Matt may just have used a form of expression that he had read used before in this way. He may even have been told by a teacher something along the lines of "*Man* in Old English meant *person*; so it includes women." Therefore, Matt may believe he is including women in his reference. If we claim that his usage is nevertheless sexist, that *man* really does not include women, we crucially assume that language can be critiqued for implications that are not necessarily under the conscious control of the speaker or writer.

However, it is not enough just to assert that these usages are biased. The problem is that the meaning appears to be hidden as much as revealed by the form. In order to justify our response, we have to make the effort to tease the meaning out. That is a lot of work, and there is the danger that we are reading too much into the language we are objecting to. Certainly, anyone whose work we are critiquing for sexism is likely to make just that claim.

If discerning sexist language is problematic, avoiding it can be as well. Many careful speakers and writers worry about using sexist terms, just as they do about other oppressive forms of expression. This concern is the other side of the presumptive coin that writers and speakers are not entirely in control of their messages. It is also a connection between sexist language critique and more traditional forms of prescription. Speakers, and especially writers, have long been concerned about the inadequacy of their abilities to express themselves generally, and these insecurities have historically been the lifeblood of prescription.

In fact, the development of traditional prescriptive grammar can be seen in large part as a mechanism for dealing with linguistic insecurity. Prescriptive grammarians codified a series of usages that they considered correct, and so provided a seemingly solid ground for arbitrating acceptability. The need for such arbitration explains the paradox of why the acceptance of "authority in language", as Milroy and Milroy (1986) put it, is still so unquestioned in a society whose dominant ideology is steeped in the notion of individual freedom. Linguistic agents – to use McConnell-Ginet's (1983) term for speakers and writers – feel safe in employing a particular word or structure if it is recommended by an authority, such as are found in a handbook, professional dictum, or language commentary.

The reliance on authority is so great that it does not appear to matter that the dictums these authorities hand down are linguistically indefensible; at least the grounds they appeal to are inevitably spurious. Pinker (1994 p. 372), for example, eloquently sums up the sort of conclusions linguists usually come to when they look at traditional grammatical prescriptions:

> One can choose to obsess over prescriptive rules, but they have no more to do with human language than the criteria for judging cats at a cat show have to with mammalian biology.

On this point, an important distinction should be made that differentiates critique of sexist language from traditional prescriptive grammar. The older tradition is covertly ideological in nature. Traditional prescription banned forms such as *she ain't* largely because they were used by the lower classes, at the same time claiming that the problem involved some kind of absolute linguistic incorrectness based on lack of agreement.[1]

Current prescription of forms deemed to give offense is, by contrast, open in its ideological aims. Terms such as *fireman* are replaced by *fire fighter* to acknowledge the fact that gender is not, or at least should not, be relevant for a description of that occupation. Finally, the ideology is out in the open, and that makes the claims open to honest debate in a way that appeals to some kind of fictitious transcendental correctness cannot be.

Nevertheless, extreme caution must be exercised to avoid being superficial and dogmatic about ideological assertions, or to make the same kinds of appeals to transcendent truth that plague traditional prescriptions. It is all too easy to declare a usage to be sexist by *fiat* just as certain usages were declared incorrect by *fiat*. It is worth making an effort to remember that there is honest room for disagreement and that simplistic assertions have the potential to make cosmetic changes and undo careful thought about language.

The kind of danger inherent in simplistic prescriptive approaches to language and sexism issues can be seen in the following anecdote involving a freshman at a community college. This student showed me a paper she had written in which the instructor had crossed out the word *sexes* and inserted *genders* in its place. In the margin her instructor wrote: "Sex refers to an act not a person." In this way, this instructor used a bit of linguistic folklore that a word *really* means something at odds with how it is actually used to justify her prescriptive comment. In doing so, she unintentionally obliterated the reason the term *gender* was adopted in social science discourse in the first place. *Gender,* after all, differentiates between socially-constructed categories, while *sex* does the same for biological ones. If *gender* is used for both concepts, we end up in the same situation we were in the first place, with no lexical way to distinguish the social from the biological. The moral of the story is that it is up to feminists and others to justify proposed changes with evidence and rational argumentation in each case.

WHAT IS IT COMMUNICATING?

If, as I say, we need to justify proposed changes rationally, not by dictum, what grounds can we appeal to? Again a look at older forms of prescription are illuminating. It is true that traditional prescription is a modern myth, essentially an interconnected network of legends such as: *between* stands for only two, do not split an infinitive, a pronoun agrees with its antecedent in number and gender. It is also true that revelation of the mythological nature of prescriptive grammar by linguists and others has had little effect. The ineffectiveness of linguists' critiques should be taken not as evidence for some perverse immunity of speakers to rational argumentation but as evidence that prescription is serving some other purpose. In fact, if one looks a bit below the folkloric surface, it is not hard to see what that purpose is.

To do that digging we need to use Matt for another thought experiment. Let's imagine that he pronounces the verb *ask* as *aks* during a class presentation. The problem with that usage, which in fact dates to Old English, is that it tells us information (*or possibly misinformation*) about his socio-economic background, his ethnicity, and his level of education. This information is distracting, and it interferes with the information he is trying to communicate in the presentation. Before I had Matt say the term, you probably had no clue regarding his background; now you might think of him as probably minority and from a lower socioeconomic background. More importantly, given the context I have provided – a class presentation – you may well think that he is unable or unwilling to conform to standard language norms.

Tracy faces a slightly different issue if she writes something like the following in a composition:

It's a good idea to, like, develop a sound recycling system.

While this use of *like* tends to cause some people to wince – the legend here is that it is sloppy or lazy – in fact, this kind of usage, called a focus marker, is not unusual in the world's languages. It is simply a new development in English, one that separates older speakers who do not employ it from younger ones who do. The problem is not the usage itself but the fact that it is in a composition where there is no precedent for it. Instead, it communicates an association with types of discourse that it is commonly found in, say, chatting with friends. The problem, like that of *aks*, is that it gives bad information, though here that information involves issues of textual identity rather than personal identity.

This point is important because only if we look past the spurious prescriptive grammatical rules, can we see that, ultimately, the problems that arise with inappropriate usages are not the forms themselves. Complaints that young people's language is sloppy or lazy, after all, go back to at least Swift. However, it is unlikely that each succeeding generation actually does use language more poorly than the preceding one since if that were the case we would be pretty much speechless by now. In other words, the language is not in decline. Usages are not correct and incorrect in and of themselves. It is just that some forms are undesirable because they have undesirable meanings of one kind or another, either in terms of what they say about our socioeconomic status, or the type of text we are producing, or both. Yet when these forms pull us towards mistaken or irrelevant conclusions regarding textual or personal identity, they provide misinformation or distracting information.

By contrast, when the forms used in a text are appropriate, they tell us nothing we did not already know about an author, and they create appropriate intertextual links. In this way they become informationally null. The paradox of language is that it is invisible when communication is running smoothly. We only examine it when some misinformation or inappropriate information draws our attention to it.

The case of sexism is not different in kind. Our attention is drawn when the language supplies unintentionally sexist information or intentionally sexist, but covert, implications.[2]

Therefore, feminist language critique can be useful to the extent that it establishes guidelines that linguistic agents can use when examining language, either their own or others', for issues of gender bias. The focus on the linguistic code implied by the expression *sexist language* makes sense only insofar as it refers to those instances when the sexism of the message is not transparently available and so needs to be ferreted out. The hidden nature of the sexism forces the reader or listener to look at the language to find the hidden message. Language is not the issue, but its use to convey sexism without appearing to is. As the feminist and linguist, Sally McConnell-Ginet (1988 p. 91), put it:

> My aim is to suggest something of the mechanisms through which social privilege leads to a kind of linguistic privilege, making it appear that the language itself supports the interests and reflects the outlook of those with privilege (by virtue of sex or class or race), and the language itself resists threats to that privilege. The appearance is not illusory, although it is not a language (an interpreted system) but language (use) that helps subordinate women (and other dominated groups).

CRITIQUING SEXIST LANGUAGE

It follows from the last section that any attempt to examine sexism in language must be focused on all the meanings of a text, particularly the covert and unintentional ones. That conclusion is fine in principle, but what exactly should a teacher do if Tracy writes the following?

> A teenager typically doesn't worry about his future.

Is that usage sexist? The answer cannot be definitively yes; we don't know the context after all, but it is probably yes. Fortunately, a number of researchers have examined the prescription of epicene *he* (the use of "he" coreferent with a singular antecedent with a referent of indeterminate sex). They have shown that the prescription was originally a product of sexism (Bodine 1975, Sklar 1983). Similarly, other research indicates that it is not really gender-neutral at all (Kidd 1972, Martyna 1983, Cochran 1988, among many others). For example, some of these studies have shown that purportedly sex-neutral generics referred to with *he* evoke male images. Others have demonstrated that when given a choice of pronoun to be used with different antecedents, linguistic agents tend to use *he* for those that display a stereotypical masculine bias. My own work shows that stereotypically male generics (e.g. lumberjacks, participants in congressional sex scandals) are referred to with the male pronoun more frequently than neutral ones are in naturalistic discourse (Newman 1997,

1998).

While some have used this and similar phenomena as evidence that English is a sexist language, it would be more reasonable to blame not the language but its misuse. Grammarians and even many linguists have tended to assimilate pronouns with other meaningless grammatical function words such as prepositions. However, there is a good deal of evidence that pronouns have not lost all their lexical value (Rigau 1986). As Lasnik (1977) suggested, "he" can simply mean male person. It follows from that common-sense view that any person indicated by *he* would be assumed to be male, much as would any person referred to by, say, *boy.*

Thus, we can tell Tracy that when she uses the male pronoun, readers are likely to make the inference, perhaps unconsciously, that the teen she is referring to is male. Furthermore, we can advise her that if we only make reference to boys when we refer to teenagers, she will be left out of the discussion. If she is convinced by these arguments and asks us what she should do, we can inform her of the results of other research. It is important to consider singular *they* as a viable alternative. Certainly, there is no rational basis for insisting that a pronoun agree in number with the antecedent, as Pinker (1994) and many others have noted. In fact, in extemporaneous speech, even in formal registers used on television programs, singular *they* dominates epicene usage and is used even in certain sex-definite cases (Newman 1997, 1998). Furthermore, as Meyers (1990) shows, it is common in the print media; therefore, it can hardly be claimed that singular *they* implies that the writer is uneducated in the way, say, the use of double negatives in writing would.

In fact, anyone who regards double negatives and singular *they* as equivalent lapses in need of immediate correction is clearly a true believer in the mythology of correctness and the transcendental nature of linguistic rules. There is little to argue about when dealing with faith. Yet it is only fair to acknowledge the use of singular *they* puts the writer at risk of censure by those who do believe that it is incorrect. This is a fact that Tracy and her teacher should also consider.

There is another complication that should be noted, a subtle linguistic point: Sexism aside, the use of a singular pronoun does not mean quite the same thing as *they*. When a singular is used, it evokes what McConnell-Ginet (1979) calls a prototype, a sort of personification of the generic referred to, whereas singular *they* implies a more purely generic or type sense. For example, imagine that Tracy replaced the *he* in the example above with *they*:

A teenager typically doesn't worry about their future.

This change may be quite useful if she wishes to make a simple generalization about teenagers; if, however, for rhetorical reasons, she would like to give her readers an imaginary teen to identify with, then, a singular pronoun is a better choice. Furthermore, because of the fact that English has one such pronoun for each sex, she must choose not so much which pronoun to use but which image to evoke – male or female. Different subtle changes of meaning would occur if Tracy were to pick any of the various avoidance strategies suggested for handling the issue of epicenes. For example, the replacement of the problematic pronoun with *the* depersonalizes the future in such a way that we are not sure whose, if anyone's future, is being disregarded:

A teenager typically doesn't worry about the future.

It could be the teen's own future, the future of country, or of the world. Similarly, pluralizing the subject prevents the use of a generic type and only makes a weaker claim about the class. No longer is "not worrying about the future" a property of teenagers; it is only a statistical fact about most of them.

Teenagers typically don't worry about their futures.

All these complications may seem daunting. Yet they are precisely the kind of choices that writers face all the time; after all, the interplay of shades of meaning is what writing is all about, and it is why it is such a challenge to do and to teach. Yet surely the discussion of whether prototypical generic teens, cooks, secretaries, presidents, doctors, or human beings are imagined to be of one sex or another is a valuable one for the writing classroom. Similarly, discussion of whether it is worth abandoning written prototypes to avoid sexism makes for a consciousness raising that is equally valuable.

A PRINCIPLE-BASED APPROACH TO PRESCRIPTION

The solution is an approach to sexism and language that involves directing discussion of meaning in writing to these issues. It is an extension of same process-oriented guidance that has come to dominate approaches to writing instruction. It employs teachers' knowledge of the issues in writing to help the student find out a way to say exactly what they want to say. Informing Tracy that "he" implies that she is referring to boys alone is an example. Elucidating other usages both individually and in a class is helpful; a mini-lesson on the sociolinguistics of gender reference would also be appropriate. When we do these kinds of activities we accomplish a lot more than simply addressing sexist language:

-
    We give students more power to decide how to express themselves because we provide them with a way of relating the language they use to their own implicit sets of standards.
- We allow for a discussion of these standards, for, in the end, it is their own standard that writers must learn to appeal to.
- We change the very nature of prescription from laying down rules that must be followed blindly to learning to critique. Prescription as critique implies a transfer of authority both in the sense of control of knowledge (i.e. an authority on a subject) and power to control behavior (authority figure) from an editor, teacher, or handbook, to the author of the piece of writing. It is as democratic as traditional prescription is authoritarian.

In sum, sexist language is not the issue, sexist meaning is, and sexist meaning cannot be dealt with by a list of approved and proscribed usages because the forms themselves are not meaningful. A new and more helpful form of prescription in the writing classroom focuses on elucidating and critiquing what writers say, looking for and exposing sexism in what they say, and helping writers ultimately decide what they are going to say.

An obvious question is how can this be done. A methodology may take the form of a limited set of principles that can serve as guidance for writers and their critics. Evidently, these principles are not going to satisfy those who want a clear checklist consisting of *no-nos* and *yes-yeses*. On the other hand, such a system in the form of traditional grammar does not work. Obviously, there are some principles that relate to clarity and honesty in language use. These are the type of issues that preoccupied Orwell as discussed in Chomsky (1986) and Milroy and Milroy (1984). To deal with these kinds of issues now would take us far from our present concerns. Instead, I will focus on three principles that deal more directly with issues of sexism and language education.

NO USAGE SHOULD TRANSGRESS
THE LINGUISTIC SYSTEM

The point seems obvious enough but the history of prescriptive grammar is full of awkward prescriptions that have resulted from misguided attempts to "improve" the linguistic system. As Pinker (1994 p. 372) says about these rules, "The very fact that they have to be drilled shows that they are alien to the natural working of the language system."

A wonderful example is epicene *he*. This form was simply declared to be gender-neutral, a claim refuted by a considerable body of research, as we have seen. Unfortunately some of those who have worried about the problem *he* creates have come up with impractical solutions. Although they were concerned about the sexism of *he*, they never challenged the basic premise that pronouns should agree with antecedents in number and gender. So instead of seeing singular *they* as evidence that this view was mistaken, they tried to abolish it. Baron (1981) describes the long history of attempts to develop a new pronoun intended to balance out the traditional concern with agreement with that of sexism. He calls this pronoun, "the word that failed":

> It is not likely that a new pronoun with ideal
> characteristics can be devised in the same way we create
> wonder drugs or market pet food. The history of the
> epicene pronoun suggests that while it may be perceived
> by some a needed word, it remains for the language in
> general an unnecessary one (Baron 1986 p. 215).

This principle, then, serves as a warning against this kind of distrust of the language as it has come down to us. Our linguistic system can be understood (admittedly simplistically) as a mental software application, which we share with the community to which we belong. We cannot simply decide that we will do a piece of authoring without a firm understanding of the manual and the eventual agreement of other owners. On this point, it is important to realize that it is a lot easier to change the lexicon, which is only a peripheral part of the system, than the grammar.

However, even in promoting lexical change caution is needed. We can make suggestions, such as "let's use *gender* to mean a socially-constructed correlate of *sex*," and these proposals may be accepted if there's a perceived need. We cannot simply announce "*sex* refers to an act, not a person." On this point, note how many successful changes to the lexicon appear almost spontaneously. *Host*, originally a male-reference term, began to encompass both genders as the difference between what *hosts* and *hostesses* were expected to do diminished. Similarly, the success of *letter carrier, server, fire fighter*, and so on reflects changes in social attitudes regarding the role of gender in these professions at the same time as they promote these changes.

The linguistic system also has a role to play in determining sexism. Note how *mailman* seems more male than *freshman*. This may be due to the fact that *man* in *mailman* is fully stressed, and therefore, the word *man*, remains pronounced as a compound. By contrast, *-man* in *freshman*, is downstressed, as a suffix, so the vowel is reduced to *schwa* when it is pronounced at all. Thus, the maleness largely disappears.

USAGE SHOULD BE SOCIOLINGUISTICALLY INFORMED

There are two important sociolinguistic considerations. The first involves the effects of violating traditional prescriptions. I discussed this issue with reference to singular *they* and will not belabor the point here. I only wish to add that the writer needs an acute awareness of who their audience is, the effects certain usages will have on that audience, and a conception of what effects are desirable. The second consideration relates to sexism directly. It is perfectly valid to criticize a writer for implying that humans, police officers, teachers, or any other profession are or should be prototypically of one gender. It is, in a sense, similar to a usage or image that implies that a prototypical human, police officer, or teacher is of one race or another. Of course, race is not revealed in pronoun reference and is somewhat harder to hide lexically; there are, for example, few professional names, such as *coolie,* that imply ethnic specificity. However, in the end the similarities outweigh the differences and both forms of prejudice in language have received considerable sociolinguistic attention in recent years.

THE AUTHORITY LIES IN THE AUTHOR

Sociolinguistically informed prescription tells us, for example, that an epicene antecedent with *he* will bias the interpretation of the referent towards the masculine. However, what it cannot tell us is that *he* should not be used with epicene antecedents. The writer has every right to use epicene *he* if for whatever reasons, he wishes to. It is not up to style guides, teachers, or editors to tell writers what to say, only to suggest, negotiate, debate, clarify, and criticize what they say.

Again the analogy with race is informative. A writer who calls an imaginary mugger Jamal and his victim, Brett, is clearly invoking powerful stereotypes. However, would the teacher want to *correct* this usage? Any response that deals with a racist message as a language issue is missing the point. Responses need to deal with the message. One might be informing the writer that hurtful and misleading stereotypes are being invoked. Another might be to say that these images so disturbed you that you would prefer not to read the piece. Yet others would be to discuss racism in class. Finally, it is possible that the writer was deliberately playing with stereotypes of this nature in order to ridicule them or use them for ironic effect, though perhaps not doing it well enough to make the irony clear. We need to think carefully before acting as censors instead of critics of material we find disturbing.

CONCLUSION

In the end, sexism like any other prejudice is not a language problem. It is merely an issue that is expressed through language. To condemn a speaker or writer's language *qua* language rather than revealing how the language expresses sexist ideas is only to condemn the messenger instead of the message. Writing and the process of critiquing the meaning of the writing is therefore a good way to become more aware of prejudices that are at times relatively hidden. The saddest thing about a simplistic, rule-based prescription on sexist issues is that it stifles the expression of problematic areas of our lives even before we begin to have a chance to discuss them and so change them. The goal of writing education should be to facilitate expression of ideas, not to teach students to hide them.

In this article I have laid out views of sexist writing that deal with meaning through form rather than with form alone. That is why you have found no lists of usages that I consider sexist, together with alternatives that could substitute for them. Does my approach make sexist language a more complex issue than a nonsexist grammar guide might have it? Yes. Does it require a greater degree of linguistic and sociolinguistic expertise on the part of writing teachers than is normally part of their training? Perhaps. Is it unrealistically idealized? No. What this approach does is put sexism and other prescriptive issues in the mainstream of language pedagogy. We know what works; let's apply it to all areas of language teaching in general, and to writing teaching in particular.

ABOUT THE AUTHOR

Michael Newman is an Assistant Professor of Linguistics at Queens College-CUNY, where he teaches courses in TESOL and sociolinguistics. He has also worked as an EFL/ESL teacher in Barcelona and New York, and as a teacher educator in New Jersey and Ohio. His current research interests include information in academic literacy and sociolinguistics.

REFERENCES

Baron, Dennis (1986). *Grammar and Gender*, New Haven Yale U.P.

Bodine, Ann (1975). "Androcentrism in prescriptive grammar: Singular 'they,' sex-indefinite 'he' and 'he or she' *Language in Society*, 4, 129-146.

Cochran, Effie (1988). Generic Masculine Pronominal Usage and Sex-Linked Occupational Stereotypes among High School Students. Doctoral Dissertation. Teachers College, Columbia University.

Crowley, Tony (1989). *Standard English and the politics of language* Champaign, Il: U. of Illinois Press.

Kidd, V. (1971). "A study of the images produced through the use of male pronouns as the generic" *Moments in Contemporary Rhetoric and Communications*, 1-2, 5-30.

Lasnik, Howard (1974). "Pronouns" *Linguistic Inquiry*.

Martyna, Wendy (1983). "Beyond the He/Man approach: the case for nonsexist language" from Thorne, Barrie; Kramarae; Cheris & Henley, Nancy (eds.) *Language, Gender and Society*. Rowley, MA: Newbury House 25-37.

McConnell-Ginet (1979). "Prototypes, Pronouns and Persons" in Mathiot, Madeleine (ed.) *Ethnolinguistics: Boas, Sapir, and Whorf revisited* The Hauge Mouton, 63-83.

McConnell-Ginet, Sally (1983). Review of Language, Sex and gender: Does 'la difference' make a difference and Sexist langauge: A modern philosphical analysis" *Language 59*: 373-391.

McConnell-Ginet, Sally (1988). "Language and Gender" in Newmeyer, Frederick (ed) *Linguistics: the Cambridge Survey Volume IV Language the Socio-cultural context*. Cambridge University Press p. 75-99.

Milroy, James. & Milroy, Leslie (1984). *Authority in language: investigating, language, prescription, and standardization*. London and NY: Routledge.

Newman, Michael (1997). *Epicene pronouns: the linguistics of a prescriptive problem*. New York: Garland.

Newman, Michael (1998). What pronouns can tell us: a case study of epicenes in English, *Studies in Language*, 22: 2 p.

Pinker, Steven (1994). *The language instinct*. NY: William Morrow.

Rigau, Gemma (1986). "Some remarks on the nature of strong pronouns in null-subject languages' in Ivonne Bordelois, Heles Contreras, Karen Zagona (eds) *Generative studies in Spanish syntax*. Dordrecht-Holland: Foris.

Sklar, Elizabeth (1983). "Sexist Grammar Revisted, " *College English*, 45, 348-358.

Smith, John (1983). "La norme linguistique chez les grammairiens de l'Inde ancienne" in Bedard, Edith & Maurais, Jacques (eds) *La norme lingistique* Quebec/Paris: Conseil de la Langue Française/Le Robert. pp. 21-44.

ENDNOTES

1. *Ain't* began as a contraction of *am not*, and the original grammarians did not object to its use as such, only to its employment as a contraction for *is not* or *are not*. The stigma associated with its first person use is much later. The spuriousness of the original argument, that *She ain't* violates subject-verb agreement, can be seen in the acceptance of the equally mismatched *aren't I?* as a question tag.

2. The problem with an overtly sexist tract is not the use of the word *man* or the exclusive pronominal reference, but the message being intentionally delivered. This is arguably not a writing issue at all.

GENDER IN PUBLIC LIFE: PEDAGOGY FOR ESL

by
Joan Lesikin
&
Alice H. Deakins
William Paterson University, New Jersey

(Annotated Resources and Sample Activity Units by Joan Lesikin)

ABSTRACT

Intended for high school, college, or adult ESOL instructors, this chapter presents a pedagogical framework for using gender themes related to the areas of education and the workplace. The themes provide students with the opportunity to reflect on their knowledge of cultural stereotypes, to consider their own individual experiences of gender role behavior, and to explore intercultural aspects of gender role behavior in public life. Assumptions about gender and diversity are outlined here, along with suggested tasks that utilize different skills. In addition, annotated resources for classroom use as well as two sample lesson units to demonstrate implementing several of the tasks are provided by Lesikin.

Gender as a topic has brought high interest, energy, and engagement to our own ESOL classes. Because everyone lives a gendered life and because so many rapid changes in the contemporary world have a gender dimension, our ESL students relish the topic. They eagerly explore aspects of gender, often assuming that the gender roles learned in their first culture are universal and unchanging. However, reality is more nuanced. The existence of gender roles is universal, but they are diverse and changing in that universality. Gender issues, therefore, provide our students with numerous opportunities to reflect on their own values and behavior.

While gender influences our behavior in many areas of our lives, in this article we focus on public life, specifically on education and work. In both areas, gender practices are often hidden but reinforced by their existence in respected public institutions such as schools and businesses.

In schools in students' native cultures, issues of gender were likely invisible, as in US schools. However, since education lays a foundation for students' futures, differing practices, patterns, and values based on gender can either impede or nurture students' visions and attainments. Thus differences based on gender need to become visible. (See Sadker & Sadker 1982, 1994, Gabriel & Smithson 1990, Orenstein 1994, Yepez 1994, AAUW 1999.) Similarly, differences based on gender are likely present in workplaces in students' own cultures, as in the US. These differences also need to be examined, since different values, diverse practices, and changing patterns related to gender in the workplace may create conflicts with colleagues, superiors, and subordinates (Case 1992, Tannen 1994, Arliss & Borisoff 1993, McElhinny 1998).

In this chapter, we (1) outline our assumptions about gender and diversity, (2) suggest tasks/activities for ESOL that use different skills in order to explore gender in education and in the workplace, (3) list some annotated resources for classroom use, and (4) present two sample lesson units in an appendix to demonstrate the implementation of some of the tasks in 2.

ASSUMPTIONS

GENDER

Gender is a universal category, but the specific traits and behaviors assigned to each gender vary from culture to culture. Generally, however, the traits and behaviors understood as appropriate to men are valued more highly in most cultures than those assigned to women. This results in *sexism*, the belief or idea that women have personalities and abilities that are different from men. As a result, in most cultures women are expected to fulfill less important roles in public life. Such sexism is often unconscious, hidden beneath the surface of our lives.

In many cultures, gender roles are changing, creating stress within cultures, families, and individuals. Many of our

ESL students are living in the midst of such change and enjoy exploring what is similar and different among cultures. By analyzing gender roles in public life we make the differences conscious, empowering students to critique the various cultures they live in and to make conscious decisions about their own values and behaviors.

STEREOTYPES AND REALITIES

The diversity of our world is visible on many levels. Most nation states are multicultural and multilingual or multidialectal. Many nations, including the United States, contain a variety of racial/ethnic groups, social classes, and languages, in addition to diversity based on education, age, gender, and sexual orientation. For each subgroup, however, stereotypes can become attached to its members; these may be positive or negative, true or untrue. These powerful stereotypes, often presented in the media, represent some people's idea of what is typical or ideal about the group.

In contrast to the narrowness of stereotypes, the world's diversity and complexity are present in our ESL students. As teachers, we ask them to reflect on both their knowledge of cultural stereotypes and their own individual experiences of gender role behavior in public life. By asking students to examine these stereotypes and realities, we hope to make visible the often hidden implications of gender related to education and the workplace.

PRESENTATION FORMAT

The tasks we present below integrate the skills of speaking, listening, viewing, reading, and writing. Although one task may focus more directly on one skill, the activities around the task promote development of other skills. The tasks vary in the type of activity students engage in: speaking (discussing, posing questions, presenting material), listening (to classmates, guest speakers), viewing (films, television, work sites, classrooms), reading (literature, advertisements, comics,

Internet sources), and writing (freewriting, questionnaires, stories, essays).

We present the tasks in the following order: reflecting, exploring, and sharing. First, we encourage wide-range thinking through freewriting and discussion (**section A**). These tasks provide opportunities for students' individual expression of gender-related experiences, feelings, and values as members of particular cultures. Next we suggest means of exploring ideas through literature, people, and media (**sections B, C, & D**). Students are able to explore gender-related experiences, feelings, values, and ideas from both inside and outside the classroom. Finally, we suggest ways of sharing what has been learned and valued in both oral and written form (**sections E & F**).

In our presentation, grammatical skills emerge from task-based activities which are based on theme and function. Some grammatical areas are general, that is, present in all activities, such as article use. Other grammatical areas emerge more specifically from particular tasks, such as questions from discussions, interviews, and questionnaires; the conditional from wish lists; tense use from writing about the past and present; auxiliary use from relating activities and states to the past and present; modal use from asking questions and writing about the future; and comparative forms from comparing various ways of experiencing gender. For those teachers who want their students to focus on specific grammatical forms, we suggest developing supplementary materials related to the activities, resources, and materials we present below.

In the discussion that follows, we present a variety of gender-based classroom activities as a survey of many, though of course not all, possibilities for exploring gender in public life. We suggest that individual teachers select only a few for classroom use, as demonstrated in the sample activity units, depending on their own interests and expertise and on the students' backgrounds and interests.

ACTIVITIES

GENDER DIFFERENCES IN EDUCATION

GOAL 1: Using student expertise to describe gender differences in education, both real and stereotypical, in students' own cultures

A. Freewriting and/or Discussion

Some suggested topics

1. In which school subjects did you do well as a primary or high school student? Which subjects did you dislike? Were these subjects typical and appropriate for your gender?

2. Recall the teachers and administrators you had in school in your own culture. Which positions did the women and men hold? Were these stereotypical female or male work roles? What personal traits made them good at their job? Are these personal traits related to gender?

3. Describe the kinds of activities girls and boys did during recess. Were they competitive or cooperative? Describe any shared activities. How did the activities reflect gender stereotyping?

4. Did any teachers show bias in favor of or against one gender? Explain how bias was displayed.

5. What was the importance or stigma of achievement and good grades for girls/boys in the primary grades and in the higher grades? Were non-conforming girls/boys labeled in any way?

6. Describe the dress codes expected or required of female and male students in your culture. Explain these codes and what they reflect about the culture's values about females and males.

7. In your culture, are students distributed by gender into specialized schools? Describe the curriculums at each school. How do the schools reflect patterns of gender stereotyping?

Wish lists

Use unreal conditional structures in order to reflect on past experiences:

1. Have students practice asking and/or answering questions in writing and/or speaking, such as:

   If you had been a female/male, what would you have *(studied/changed/done differently)*? If you had been a female/male, what *(goals, sports, pastimes, etc.)* would you have tried?

2. For less-skilled students, have them first complete partial sentences at various difficulty levels:

   ***(study)* If I were male/female, I *(would study)* . . .**
   ***(be a /baseball player* [person of a particular occupation]*)* I*(would have been a baseball player)* if I had been male/female. (Extend the sentence to include a *because* clause.)**

B. Literature
(see Annotated Resources at the end of Gender Differences in Education)

Use the following as cloze exercises, reading/speaking exercises, or for discussion:

1. Ask students to contribute literary works about education, such as short stories, essays, school anthems, songs, pledges, or cheers for athletic events. Review them for issues of gender.

2. Use students' own writing developed from the freewriting topics above (from present or past semester classes) or from formal writing pieces below as reading for subsequent students.

C. People as Resources

Questionnaires

Have students develop their own or complete teacher-made questionnaires. They can examine gender stereotyping, expectations, and exceptions to stereotyping in education in their own and classmates' cultures. Some topics are: dress codes, aspirations, after-school activities, and adult influences as role models and counselors. (Also use topics from A: Freewriting and/or Discussion.)

Interviews

Using the questionnaires developed above, either invite a guest from another culture for students to interview or have students interview someone from their culture but of an older generation.

D. Media
(see Annotated Resources at the end of Gender Differences in Education)

Comics

Have students create their own comic strips to display stereotypical, real, or exceptional gender roles that might be found in their culture's schools.

E. Presentations

Role-plays

Conflict and characters are supplied without resolution. Give each actor a card with the description of the scenario and their character. (Cards for the first role-play are given below.) Two role-plays of the same scenario but with gender-reversed roles can be done simultaneously by bisecting the class into two audiences. Both groups then unite to discuss their reactions: if and how gender or gender expectations played a part and how comfortable the audience felt about what they saw.

A female/male student wishes to study engineering/nursing, a field in her/his culture limited to men/women. The school guidance counselor opposes her/his goal because it does not conform to gender expectations. Together they discuss their views to resolve the matter.

1. _Female/male student card:_ You wish to study engineering/ nursing, a field culturally restricted to women/men. You meet your guidance counselor to discuss your plans.

2. _Guidance counselor card:_ In discussing academic and career plans, you are determined to guide the student into a career suitable to her/his gender and academic abilities.

A female/male student received a B+ on a written exam in her/his major but thinks she/he deserves an A. She/he knows that two female/male students already requested grade changes and got them. The teacher needs to be convinced that she/he is deserving. Career goals would convince the teacher.

Games

Have each student teach the class or describe a childhood game or pastime played primarily by one gender in the student's culture. Then have classmates guess which gender plays the game and later have them discuss what each game teaches about gender. In advance, the teacher can teach a game or show pictures of US examples: having a tea party [girls], playing war [boys], or playing chess [neutral].

F. Formal Writing
(see also [A] **Freewriting** and/or **Discussion**).

Some suggested topics

1. In your opinion, what were the most significant issues of gender that affected you as a school child? Consider academic, artistic, and recreational experiences. If you were given the opportunity now to speak with teachers and counselors, what advice would you give them?

2. In terms of gender, how is your culture's educational system changing or remaining the same?

3. Imagine that you are writing a **UNICEF** report on gender equity in your culture's educational system. What are the system's strengths and weaknesses and your suggestions for change?

GOAL 2: Exploring gender differences in education, both real and stereotypical, in the US

A. Freewriting and/or Discussion

Some suggested topics

1. As a female/male student, what were your greatest concerns about schooling in the US when you first arrived? Were they borne out? Explain.

2. What opportunities in US schools seem unavailable to your gender in schools in your culture? Conversely, what opportunities exist in your culture's schools but not in the US?

3. What educational and career goals do you now have? Does gender play a part in your choices? Explain. Would you have selected these same goals in your own culture? Why or why not?

4. Do teachers and students in the US expect certain behavior from you because you are female/male? If so, how do you feel about their expectations or lack of expectations? Explain.

5. How do the US school athletic programs for women and men compare to those in your culture? How do you feel about females/males taking part in highly competitive school sports?

6. What stereotypes about US female/male students do people in your culture have? Based on your experience with US education, are these stereotypes accurate?

Wish lists

To use real conditional structures in order to express wishes and desires, have students complete:

1. If I were a female/male American student in the US, I would . . .

2. If I could change one behavior of US female/male students, it would be that they . . .

3. If I were asked to give advice on *(educational goals, career goals, being on a sports team, getting more help from the teacher)* to a *(student, athlete, teacher, coach, friend, new immigrant)* of the same/other gender in the US, I'd say. . .

B. Literature
(see Annotated Resources at the end of Gender Differences in Education)

Short stories, novels, or magazine articles

Have students read essays or stories about female and male students and decide whether they would act or react the same if the protagonist's gender is changed. What gender stereotypes in a character's role, expectations, behavior, goals, conflicts, etc. might the author be relying upon?

C. People as Resources

Observation

Have students observe two classes for one period each, one taught by a US female and one by a US male. In advance, supply or have students create a list of behaviors to observe. *Some teacher behaviors to observe are:* (1) how many times the teacher calls on female/male students, (2) how much uninterrupted speaking time the teacher gives to female/male students, (3) what the teacher does when female/male students interrupt the teacher or each other. *Some student behaviors to observe are:* (1) how many female/male hands are raised each time the teacher asks a question, (2) where female/male students are seated, (3) how female/male students get the teacher's attention (e.g. calling out, raising hands), (4) how many times female/male students interrupt the teacher or each other. Students then collate their data, draw conclusions, and make recommendations in terms of gender differences and similarities in the classroom.

D. Media
(see Annotated Resources at the end of Gender Differences in Education)

Comics

To examine gender role stereotypes, have students bring in US comic strips/books of classroom behavior and guess what is stereotypical. Whiteout all or some of the dialogue and have students fill in the missing portions.

Video viewing

Using a video of a movie, TV program, or an actual US classroom, have students use the items in C. <u>People as Resources</u> above to analyze classroom behaviors. Then have students draw conclusions about classroom gender equity and make recommendations if changes are needed.

E. Presentations

1. Supply crayons, colored pencils, and collage materials for students to create portraits of the stereotypical US female and male student. Have students write captions to explain them.

2. Have students create videos to inform foreigners about gender issues in schooling in the US.

F. Formal Writing
(*see also* [A] *above*)

Some suggested topics

1. Describe gender bias in US education that you have experienced, observed, or heard about.

2. Argue for or against competitive sports and its values in terms of gender.

3. If students have observed classes (*see* [C] *People as Resources above*), have them compare the similarities and differences between the two teachers and/or between female and male students.

4. Describe what you like most/least about US female and male students or teachers.

GOAL 3: Examining conflicts resulting from differences related to gender in educational experiences in the US and in other cultures

A. Freewriting and/or Discussion

Some suggested topics

1. What is or has been difficult for you to adjust to (e.g. educational opportunity, career training, required courses, dress code, behavior expectations) as a female/male student in the US?

2. If you could change one thing about the way female/male students are treated in US schools, what would that be? Is there anything from your own culture that you would replace it with?

3. What are the characteristics of an ideal teacher in your culture? Are they different for females and males? Compare these characteristics to female and male teachers you have had in the US.

4. Recall a difficult or embarrassing moment in your schooling in the US that resulted from conflict or misunderstanding based on cultural differences in gender expectations. Was the conflict resolved? What did you learn from the experience?

5. How do female/male students in your culture behave in school-related spaces such as lines, classrooms, hallways, playgrounds, and cafeterias, compared to female/male students in the US?

6. Compare school experiences of female and male students in the US and your culture regarding: (a) where touching on the body in public is acceptable and by whom, (b) who can tease and what the limits are (i.e. name calling, remarks about dress or body), (c) who occupies more spaces.

7. What behaviors in schools are considered sexually harassing in your culture? In the US?

B. Literature

(see Annotated Resources at the end of Gender Differences in Education)

Essay

1. Have students read about immigrant or foreign students' experience in US schools to consider: (a) Are the experiences gender-specific and (b) What in the characters' actions or thoughts seem stereotypical, real, and atypical? What are the reactions to these actions or thoughts?

2. In an essay on gender expectations in education, have students highlight in different colors expectations that seem similar to and different from their own and then discuss their perceptions.

C. People as Resources

Observation

During one week, have students note down incidents of violence in the school and whether females or males are the perpetrators or the victims. From notes, have students develop charts for class presentations or discussion and then suggest ways to reduce violence in the school by writing letters to school administrators or articles for the school newspaper.

Guest speaker

Invite former ESL students and/or US students of diverse backgrounds to participate in a panel on gender issues in US schools. Examine topics related to perceived differences in behavior in settings such as classrooms, library, hallways, cafeteria, and at events such as assemblies and sport activities. Have students discuss problems and solutions for behaviors of (1) female/male US students toward female/male ESL students, (2) teachers toward female/male US students and female/male ESL students, or (3) female/male ESL students toward female/male US students.

D. Media

Videos

To inform and convince students of both genders in their native countries of alternative educational possibilities, have student groups make their own video advertisements of their ideal gender-fair school. Have students raise gender-based issues peculiar to their cultures' practices.

E. Presentations

Role-plays

Before presenting their role-play to the class, the actors decide upon a resolution to one of the conflicts below. Then the audience can discuss the merits and shortcomings of the resolution.

1. The female/male teacher in the US places her hand on a male/female student's shoulder. This act is not appropriate in the student's culture. Role-play the student telling his/her teacher.

2. A female wants to play intramural basketball, but her culture is against women wearing scanty uniforms in public. Role-play the student and her parents discussing and resolving the issue.

3. A female student raises her hand frequently but is never called upon by the teacher. Role play the female student trying to resolve the issue with the teacher.

Debate

Students select differences in gendered educational experiences between the US and their cultures. They then debate the merits and demerits of these different practices.

F. Formal Writing

(see also [A] above)

Some suggested topics

1. Consider the short and long-term effects of gender inequalities in education for females or males.

2. Compare the ways female/male students in the US and in your culture express their individuality in terms of dress, hair, makeup, movement, and body adornments such as jewelry and tattoos.

3. Compare the behavior of American female and/or male students to those in your culture in specific educational settings (e.g. classrooms, library, hallways, cafeteria).

4. Consider how US females and males address and talk to their teachers versus their friends compared to your culture. Which behaviors do you prefer and why?

5. Write a letter to a friend in your country about the differences and similarities between female/male (students/athletes/teachers/coaches/friends) in the US and your culture.

6. You are a consultant to your school. Make recommendations for a more gender-equal educational environment drawing upon educational experiences in the US and in other cultures.

7. A US female/male teacher plans to go to your country to teach for a year. Make recommendations related to gender in education based on your experiences of both cultures.

8. If you or a friend have experienced sexual harassment, describe what happened, what you did about it, and how you felt as a result of your experiences.

9. Select incidences of school violence that you have observed and recommend ways to reduce it.

(For an example of a gender-based activity unit on education see the appendix).

ANNOTATED RESOURCES:
GENDER DIFFERENCES IN EDUCATION

([1] intermediate, [2] high intermediate/low-advanced, [3] advanced)

Literature

ESL materials and essays

[2] Atwan, R. (Ed.). (1997). *America now*. Boston, MA: Bedford Books. With tasks.

> Epstein, K. (1996). The classroom gender balance: Who speaks more, men or women? A senior discusses women and men speaking in class, and makes reference to men's power and privilege. 650 wds.

> Tannen, D. (1994). Gender gap in cyberspace. The difference between women's and men's approaches to computers. 1080 wds.

[2] Cisneros, S. (1995). Only daughter. In P. Gay. *Developing writers* (2nd ed.). Belmont, CA: Wadsworth. Author's Mexican father's negative view about women going to college vs. her own desire. 1250 wds.

[2] Datesman, M. K., Crandall, J., & Kearny, E. N. (1997). Chap. 9: Education in the United States. *The American ways: An introduction to American culture* (2nd ed.). Upper Saddle River, NJ: Prentice Hall Regents. Origins, description and values reflected in divers aspects of US schooling; with glossary and a large variety of student tasks (some on gender bias and cultural comparisons). 3830 wds.

[3] Marshall, P. (1983, 1993). From *Poets in the kitchen*. In S. Gillespie & R. Singleton (Eds.), *Across cultures: A reader for writers* (2nd ed.). Boston, MA: Allyn and Bacon. The influence of women's talk on the author's development. For exploring learning as gendered experiences. 3770 wds.

[2] Park, S.(1990,1994). Don't expect me to be perfect. In H. Knepler, M. Knepler, & K Kane, *Crossing cultures: Readings for composition* (4th ed.). New York: Macmillan College. Parental pressure to do well at school on a Korean female student. For exploring gendered, cross-cultural expectations. With reading and writing tasks. 500 wds.

[3] Wiener, H.S., & Bazerman, C. (Eds.). (1996). *Side by side: A multicultural reader* (2nd ed.).Boston, MA: Houghton Mifflin. With key words; discussion, reading and writing tasks.

Morgan, J. 'Those loud black girls.' Study of failure in college of high-achieving black women suggests gender norms may differ in black and white females. 940 wds.

Scott, J. (1994). Boys only: Separate but equal? Single sex education for African American boys to counter the perceived clash between the male culture of young black boys and the female-dominated culture they encounter at home and in school. 2250 wds.

Fairy tales, legends, myths and traditional stories

[2] The creation of the Crow world [Crow legend]. (1993). In S. Gillespie & R.Singleton (Eds.),*Across cultures: A reader for writers* (2nd ed.). Boston, MA: Allyn and Bacon. Old Man as teacher; Crows as students. For examining gender expectations and labor divisions. 660 wds.

Novels and historical works

[1] Forbes, K. (1943, 1971). *Mama's bank account*. New York: Harcourt Brace Jovanovich. A Norwegian immigrant family adjusts to American school and community values due to the mother's good management and the father's perseverance. 147 pp.

Gay, P. (Ed.). (1995). Chap. 4: Going to college: Educational histories. In *Developing writers* (2nd ed.). Belmont, CA: Wadsworth.

[3] Palmer, B. (1897). Segment of commencement address. 2500 wds.

[3] Rich, A. (1979). Commencement address. Education is understanding how men perceive and organize knowledge, women students should demand serious attention. 1800 wds.

[3] Tarbell, I. M. (1929,1985). A will to freedom from *All in the day's work*. She chooses to go to college and remain a spinster to attain equality. 850 wds.

[2] Yezierska, A. (1925). College. A female immigrant adjusts to college life while working manually.

[1] McGovern, A., & Goodwin, H.(Illus.). (1975/1990). *The secret soldier: The story of Deborah Sampson*. New York: Scholastic. A poorly educated girl becomes a diarist and teacher; disguised as a teenage boy, she becomes a soldier in the American Revolution. Juvenile book. See pp. 11-14 on females not being allowed schooling even if they begged for it. 64 pp.

[1] Monsell, H. A., & Fiorentino, A.(Illus.). (1986). *Susan B. Anthony Champion of women's rights*. New York: Aladdin. Focus on Anthony's childhood. Juvenile book. See pp. 85-97 on the measures taken to prevent females from learning math in the one-room schoolhouse.192 pp.

Poetry

[1] Brooks, G. (1996). Sadie and Maud. In B. Dyer, *Power play: Individuals in conflict*. Upper Saddle River, NJ: Prentice Hall Regents. One sister went to college; the other stayed at home; with glossary and reading, discussion and writing tasks. 20 lines.

[1] Glenn, M. (1982). Billy Paris. In *Class dismissed! High school poems*. New York: ClarionBooks/Ticknor & Fields. After his Spanish teacher announces, "No snacking while speaking Spanish," Billy brings a tablecloth, candles, bowl, and thermos of soup and names every object in a perfect Spanish accent. For exploring gendered school behaviors. 20 lines.

Vendler, H. (1997). *Poems, poets, poetry: An introduction and anthology*. Boston, MA: Bedford Books.

[2] Brooks, G. We real cool. Young black school dropouts. 8 lines.

[3] Dove, R. Flash cards. A father overworks his 10-year-old daughter in math drills. 14 lines.

[2] Glück, L. The school children. A mother's view of the first day of school. 14 lines.

[3] Snyder, G. Axe handles. An ax and handle as a metaphor of a father-son relationship and teaching/learning. 36 lines.

Proverbs

"Knowledge is power." (F. Bacon)

"If at first you don't succeed, try and try again."

"The many-sided mind is ripe for every prize." (M. Tupper)

"Reading maketh a full man, conference a ready man, and writing an exact man." (F. Bacon)

Short stories

[2] Jackson, S. (1948, 1968). Charles. In G. McHargue (Ed.), *The best of both worlds*. Garden City: NY: Doubleday. Starting kindergarten is so hateful that a boy acts out at school but brings tales about an awful Charles home. For exploring gendered school behaviors/expectations. 370 wds.

Media

Magazines and newspapers

Comics and cartoons such as those by Matt Groening and Jules Feiffer are useful and found in collected works such as:

Heller, S.(Ed.). (1982). *Jules Feiffer's America*. New York: Alfred A. Knopf.

Groening, M.(1987). *School is hell*. New York: Pantheon Books. Groening, M.(1990). *The big book of hell*. New York: Pantheon Books. Articles in professional journals such as *Kappa Delta Pi Record* contain readable articles on education for ESL students.

Movies on video

Dangerous minds. (1995 US). 95 min. A new teacher in a Los Angeles high school learns to cope with intelligent but troubled students.

Dead poets society. (1989 US). 128 min. In 1959 a charismatic teacher inspires his impressionable, all-male prep students. For discussing gender roles, expectations and male friendships.

Prime of Miss Jean Brodie, The. (1969 UK). 116 min. In a 1930's Scotland girls' school, a teacher inspires her female pupils. Compare boys' behaviors, activities and values in *Dead poets society*.

Scent of a woman. (1992 US). 137 min. A blind, womanizing, retired military officer on a NYC weekend. See male values in school trial and older-younger male friendships scenes.

Stand and deliver. (1988 US). 104 min. A dedicated teacher inspired his dropout prone students to learn calculus to build their self-esteem; they do so well that they are accused of cheating.

To sir, with love. (1967 UK). 105 min. In London, a new teacher teaches respect to his rude students, gets involved in their lives, deals with an amorous student's advances and wins over the bully.

Yentl. (1983 US). 134 min. Based on an Isaac Bashevis Singer story, a young Eastern European woman at the turn of the century impersonates a boy in order to get an education.

Television shows

Current shows and reruns present scenes of school, such as: *Family Matters; Sabrina, the Teenage Witch; Boy Meets World; The Wonder Years*.

ACTIVITIES

GENDER DIFFERENCES IN THE WORKPLACE

GOAL 1: Using student knowledge to describe gender differences in the workplace, both real and stereotypical, in students' own cultures

A. Freewriting and/or Discussion

Some suggested topics

1. What are the traditional jobs done only by women or done only by men in your culture? Describe them. Why are they limited to a single gender? Are there differences between urban and rural workers? (Or are there differences based on social class as well as gender?) Explain.

2. Where do educated (or working-class) women and men perform their traditional jobs? What are the working conditions? Do they receive money or other forms of payment for work?

3. Are there any traditional jobs done by both women and men? Explain.

4. At what age do people enter the work force in your culture? How does it vary by gender, by setting (urban/rural), and by social class?

5. How do family responsibilities such as child-care, housework, and care for the elderly fit into the traditional work patterns for women and men?

6. What are some stereotypes about female and male workers in your culture? Are they accurate?

7. Define sexual harassment. Discuss whether it is an issue in the workplace in your culture.

B. **Literature**
   (see Annotated Resources at the end of Gender Differences in the Workplace)

1. Have students examine textbooks or children's literature to determine the occupations females and males are represented doing. Do these represent traditional or non-traditional roles?

2. Have students examine annual reports of international corporations to learn the percentage of men and women serving as officers and on executive boards and their responsibilities.

3. Have students make a list of job names in their language that are gender specific like waiter/waitress and that are gender-neutral like firefighter. Then have students search in their dictionary for gender neutral forms or have them invent them if none exist.

4. Have students name titles and terms of address for peers, subordinates, and superiors at workplaces in their cultures to discuss what any gender differences in these labels reveal.

C. **People as Resources**

Interviews

Have students interview a person who works or has worked in another culture on topics such as:

(1) gendered division of labor, including which is more prestigious; (2) changing patterns of gendered and non-gendered labor; (3) awareness of sexual harassment and means of addressing it; (4) gendered differences in compensation and benefits; (5) family obligations such as child-care, housework, and eldercare in relation to occupational demands; (6) stereotypes of temporary or seasonal female/male workers from other cultures.

D. Media

(see Annotated Resources at the end of Gender Differences in the Workplace)

Help-wanted advertisements

Have students read ads from their cultures to determine if gender preference is present. Which types of jobs prefer females and which males?

Product advertisements

Have students discuss the representations of jobs that females and males are portrayed as doing in ads from their cultures. Do they appear to slot females and males into particular occupations?

Video viewing

Have students view and analyze videos from non-US cultures for workplace gender differences.

E. Presentations

Role-play

Have two students role-play a male supervisor criticizing a female subordinate for coming to work late. Then have two other students reverse the roles. Afterwards have students react to both role-plays in terms of reasonableness, realism and probability, and their own comfort with the roles.

Questionnaires

Have students present the results of their interviews to the class.

F. Formal Writing

(see also [A] on previous page)

Some suggested topics

1. Compare female and male occupations in terms of one or several of the following: setting (rural/urban), class, age, race/ethnicity.

2. Suggest and explain recommendations for workplace changes for women, men, or children.

3. Describe the differences between urban and rural work for women and men. In your opinion, who has the more difficult burden?

4. Compare the working conditions of women and men based on social class.

5. Select an occupation done traditionally by women and one done traditionally by men. Then compare them in terms of skill, fulfillment, compensation, etc.

6. Explain the differences between traditional occupations done solely by one gender and those done by either gender.

7. Compare the traditional work patterns for women and men to newer work patterns in relation to child-care, housework, and care for the elderly.

8. Discuss sexual harassment in the workplaces in your culture and means of dealing with it.

9. Write a story about someone who was sexually harassed at the workplace in your culture.

GOAL 2: Exploring gender differences, both real and stereotypical, in US workplaces

A. Freewriting and/or Discussion

Some suggested topics

1. What do you consider to be high- and low-status jobs in the US? Explain how gender seems to interact with status as possible reasons for assigning particular jobs high or low status.

2. Discuss jobs you have had in the US. Were there any gender differences in jobs open to women and men in terms of dress code, titles and terms of address, benefits and compensation?

3. Define sexual harassment. Describe any experiences that you have observed which you consider sexual harassment in the workplace. Is it usually between equals or between subordinates and superiors? Why? Is it usually males harassing females or the reverse? Explain.

4. Which would you rather have, a female or male boss? Why?

5. Do co-workers seem to socialize and date outside the workplace in the US? Explain whether you think socializing with and dating co-workers are good practices.

B. Literature

Have students create a men's magazine modeled on *Cosmopolitan* or another magazine for working women. Have students rewrite articles making appropriate changes, altering illustrations, inserting appropriate advertisements, etc.

C. People as Resources

Guest speaker

Ask the school's career counselor to speak to the class about workplace gender issues: resume writing, interviewing, job searches, career opportunities, learning one's aptitudes and interests.

Class trip

Arrange a class trip or have student pairs go to both a blue-collar and a white-collar workplace where they may observe a division of labor. Ask them to describe and rate the importance of what women and men employees are each doing. Then have students write about their observations.

D. Media
(see Annotated Resources at the end of Gender Differences in the Workplace.)

Television or video viewing

Use US work scenes of women/men in positions of power/ subservience to compare perspectives on:

1. The jobs American women and men are shown doing, how they seem to feel about them, how successful they are, and how their success seems to be measured.

2. Portrayals of working women and men in terms of work practices among colleagues, superiors, and inferiors: How is conflict resolved, who orders whom and how is it done, how are praise and criticism handled, what dress and behavior codes are observed at work.

3. Portrayals of male/female partners: How each balances a job and their relationship, including the distribution of work in the home, attitudes towards the partner's work, relative workplace success of each.

Advertisements

Bring in or have students collect ads that show men and women at work. Have students categorize them according to gender, job status, and product being marketed or service rendered. Students can also categorize the ads according to traditional and non-traditional work roles.

E. Presentations

Video

After having students formulate guidelines on sexual harassment, have students create a video on sexual harassment guidelines for the workplace.

Role-plays

In the following, the conflict and roles are given, but the viewpoints of each are kept secret from other actors, the outcome is not supplied, and a resolution must be reached to end the role-plays.

1. A female/male employee must ask for time off for eldercare. The company has no policy.

   - *The boss*: sympathetic but concerned about who will do the employee's work, willing to give the employee two weeks off.

   - *The employee*: resolved to quit if the boss does not give her a month off.

2. Wanting to file a sexual harassment grievance against a co-worker, a female/male employee speaks to the boss. The co-worker keeps leaving racy, suggestive jokes on her/his desk.

   - *The employee*: upset and offended by the co-worker.

   - *The boss*: friend of co-worker and source of jokes; didn't know co-worker passed them on.

3. A worker keeps leaving early (at 4 instead of 5 PM) to care for her/his school-age child. The boss has made an appointment to speak to the worker.

- **The boss:** wants to keep talented worker but cannot have worker leaving early.

- **The worker:** must keep job but must attend to child.

4. A female/male salesclerk wants to sell men's/women's clothing, work reserved in the store up to now for males/females. She/he is meeting with the boss.

- **The female/male clerk:** tired of selling women's/men's clothing and accessories, wants larger commissions given in men's/women's department.

- **The boss:** thinks it's inappropriate for a person to work in a department catering to the other gender but hates to lose valued salesclerk.

Brochure

A company employing 200 workers has no policy on employees taking time off for pregnancy, child-care, or eldercare. Have groups research on-line or in the library what policies are practiced and then create a company brochure to advertise its new policies to prospective employees.

F. Formal Writing
(see also [A] above)

Some suggested topics

1. Using questions related to gender problems in the workplace gleaned from advice columns in newspapers or magazines (such as Ann Landers), have students write advice letters.

2. Describe a job experience you have had where gender-related issues occurred.

3. Discuss the benefits of a female or male boss.

4. Based on your reading or your own experience or the experience of someone you know, define sexual harassment and provide examples.

5. Compare high- and low-status jobs in the US and the interaction of gender.

6. Argue for or against an employee's right to paid care-taking leave for the birth or adoption of a child, for a sick family member, or for an aging parent.

7. Argue for or against dating someone who works at the same place you do.

GOAL 3: **Examining changing patterns in the workplace related to gender in students' own cultures and US cultures**

A. Freewriting and/or Discussion

Some suggested topics

1. Are the women and men of your generation working at different jobs than the women and men of previous generations? Explain. Describe the jobs women can but do not very often do in your culture. Why don't they?

2. What are considered prestigious professions in your culture? Are both women and men in positions of authority in these professions in your culture?

3. What is considered non-prestigious work in your culture? Are both genders doing it? Explain. If there are positions of authority, are both genders performing these jobs in your culture?

4. If both partners in a relationship are working, who does child care, elder care, and housework?

5. Do women and men serve in the military or perform service to the country? Explain the obligation and reasons for being excused. Relate these to the culture's values for each gender.

6. Would you date someone who works at the same place you do? Why or why not?

7. Define sexual harassment according to your culture's expectations of workplace behavior. What protections exist and what changes would you like to see introduced? Why?

8. How should a person being sexually harassed in the workplace respond?

B. Literature
(see Annotated Resources at the end of Gender Differences in the Workplace.)

1. Have students locate readings translated into English on work-related subject matter from their cultures from an earlier time or supply a story or fairy tale to the class. Then have students examine the occupational titles, the status of the work and workers depicted, and the concerns/conflicts and resolutions presented. Have students then create a more contemporary story.

2. As a class, have students review US anthologies containing work-related subject matter. Students can compare changes in gendered roles in work across US cultures and across times.

3. Have students read a story about a worker and write a letter to the worker's superior or inferior suggesting changes in the worker's circumstances.

C. People as Resources

Interviews

1. Have students interview the human resources director at either a public institution or a private corporation to learn what changes have taken place in relation to gender: job opportunities and advancement, salary, benefits, protection, harassment policies and practices, etc.

2. Have students interview a worker about how gender is an issue in their workplace: language, appropriateness of dress, pictures on walls, non-verbal behavior, tasks, supervision, etc.

3. Have students interview a female or male in a job traditionally reserved for their gender that is now open to the opposite gender, such as: firefighter, police officer, nurse, carpenter. How does this person feel and deal with the job, co-workers, superiors, and inferiors?

D. Media

Television viewing

Use a program in which women or men are in non-traditional work roles to analyze points such as:

1. *The laugh track:* What is the programmer suggesting is funny to the viewing audience? Is any of the humor based on gender role reversal?

2. *The story:* Is the plot related to the reversal of gender roles?

3. *The characters:* Are these stereotypical or non-traditional gender roles?

Magazines

1. Have students examine magazines marketed to working women, such as *Working Women,* for articles addressing gender-related issues at the workplace. Have students discuss how they feel about these issues and whether these or other issues would be relevant in their own cultures.

2. Have students select and then change a work-related article found in a woman's magazine to make it suitable for a men's magazine.

3. Have students bring in ads containing illustrations of workers from US magazines and those from their cultures. Have groups organize the ads according to gender and job status. Have them discuss: In what kinds of jobs are women and men portrayed? What do the ads reveal about the changing nature of gendered work in their own cultures and US culture?

E. Presentations

Role-plays

1. One student group are the workers, another group are the managers of a large corporation. They are negotiating a three-year contract. (For a simulation, add other roles such as owner, negotiators for each side, arbitrator, and board members.) Use one or more issues, such as: day care, maternity/paternity leave, personal days and health insurance coverage. Each side must decide: (1) Who will pay, worker, employer, or will it be divided between them? Why? and (2) What will be the exact benefits?

2. Each role-play below has one point of conflict and ends when a resolution is reached. Each actor's reason is to be divulged during the role-play. The actors are to fill out details of their characters' lives. Some issues are:

    - *Cost sharing of day care by employee/employer*

    In favor: Can't afford to pay for private day care for two children.

    Against: Can't afford to have more money taken out of paycheck.

    - *Maternity/paternity leave*

    In favor: Both spouses work. They want to begin a family soon and share childcare.

    Against: Men are not caregivers.

    - *Personal days to nurture spouse/children*

    In favor: Married with school-age children but live far from relatives.

    Against: Married with school-age children and live near relatives.

- *Health insurance coverage of more gynecological services at higher premium*

In favor: Wants additional coverage because reaching age 50.

Against: Refuses to pay for something that will not be used.

3. A panel of student judges must decide if behaviors such as those below are considered sexual harassment and, if so, recommend an appropriate redress. After each case, students give an explanation of their verdict. Two groups of judges can each deal concurrently with a female and male plaintiff in the reverse situation to provide a comparison of whether the verdicts were gender-influenced.

    - An executive, the plaintiff, notices that every time she/he meets with the male/female vice president, his eyes scan her/his body as she/he discusses business.

    - A male/female manager puts sexual cartoons or suggestive pictures on a female/male employee's desk for her/him, the plaintiff, to see.

    - A female/male employer makes sexual comments and innuendoes about other people when the plaintiff, a male/female, is present.

F. **Formal Writing**
(see also [A] above)

Some suggested topics

1. Argue for/against women in more traditional male jobs and males in more traditional female jobs.

2. Compare child-care arrangements now to traditional child-care arrangements in your culture.

3. Compare changes related to your family and work obligations since coming to the US.

4. Argue for or against women serving in the military in the same capacity as men.

5. Compare your current or expected work life in the US with what your same-gender relatives and friends are doing in your country. What are the advantages and disadvantages of each?

6. Compare your jobs before you came to college with the ones that you expect to have afterward.

7. Compare sexual harassment awareness and management in your country and in the US.

(For an example of a gender-based activity unit on the workplace, see the appendix.)

ANNOTATED RESOURCES:
GENDER DIFFERENCES IN THE WORKPLACE

([1] intermediate, [2] high intermediate/low-advanced,[3] advanced)

Literature

ESL materials and essays

[1] Ackert, P. (1999). Lesson 3: Women and change. In *Cause & effect: Intermediate reading practice* (3rd ed.). Boston, MA: Heinle & Heinle. Research suggests that women may do more than their share of work; with 6 pp. of reading, writing, grammar tasks. 625 wds.

[2] Chisholm, S. (1970, 1981). Selection from *Unbought and unbossed* In K. A. Blake & M. L. McBee (Eds.). *Essays* (2nd ed.). New York: Macmillan. Comments on stereotyping and reflects on being black and being female as her "handicaps." 425 wds.

[2] Datesman, M. K., Crandall, J., & Kearny, E. N. (1997). Chap. 6: The world of American business. *The American ways: An introduction to American culture* (2nd ed.). Upper Saddle River, NJ: Prentice Hall Regents. Description and values reflected (e.g., competition, prestige); with glossary, various tasks (some topics on working women's issues, gender bias and cultural comparisons). 2900 wds.

[2] Genasci, L. (1995,1996). Barriers fall for women at work. In B. Wegmann, M. P. Knezevic, & M. Bernstein, Chap. 7: Work, *Mosaic two: A reading skills book* (3rd ed.). New York: McGraw Hill. With various tasks. Several reasons why the number of women in non-traditional jobs, the trades, is slowly increasing. 785 wds.

[3] Gordon, S. (1991). Women at risk. In *Prisoners of men's dreams: Striking out for a new feminine future*. Boston, MA: Little, Brown and Co. Women's workplace gains as traditionally defined by men is at the expense of devaluing caring work. 3000 wds.

[3] Keen, S. (1991,1996). The price of success. In A. Cassebaum & R. Haskell, *American culture and the media*. Boston, MA: Houghton Mifflin. Describes and analyzes the cost to men's body and spirit by the hidden, unwritten rules that govern corporate and professional success. 1720 wds.

[3] Knepler, H., Knepler, M., & Kane, K. (1994). *Crossing cultures: Readings for composition* (4th ed.). New York: Macmillan College. With word list, questions for discussion, reading, and writing.

> Buruma, I. (1986). Conformity and individuality in Japan. The Japanese rites of human relations place conformity over individualism, skill over originality, style over substance. 2660 wds.

> Ehrenreich, B., & Fuentes, A. (1981). Life on the global assembly line. The negative results for Third-world women working for multinational corporations. 3720 wds.

> Hines, W. (1983). Hello, Judy. I'm Dr. Smith. The habit "of medical professionals, usually male, of addressing female patients by their first names while . . . expecting to be respectfully addressed by their titles and last names." 770 wds.

[1] Raimes, A. (1987). Part III, Section 3: Work. *Exploring through writing: A process approach to ESL composition*. New York: St. Martin's. With questions.

> Kagan, J. (1983). Work in the 1980s and 1990s. Workplace satisfiers and motivators for women and men; 2 charts of top 10 of each in blue and white-collar jobs by gender. 1100 wds.

> Ahl, D. H. (1984). Dulling of the sword. Effect of romantic love on Japanese work ethic. 730 wds.

[1] Sökmen, A., & Mackey, D. (1998). *Kaleidoscope 2: Reading and writing*. Boston, MA: Houghton Mifflin.

> Chap. 14: Take your daughter to work day. 7 pp. With related tasks.

> Chap. 17: Would I work? Job announcements, a report on people's preferences to work vs. staying at home; gender-based poll. 11pp. with related tasks.

[3] Steinem, G. (1995). The importance of work. In P. A. Eschholz & A. F. Rosa (Eds.), *Outlooks and insights: A reader for college writers* (4th ed.). New York: St. Martin's Press. Women's work as a human right and as a natural and pleasurable activity. 2150 wds.

[3] Terkel, S. (1980, 1999). *American dreams: Lost and found*. New York: Ballantine Books. Edited oral histories (approx. 2000 wds. ea.) of various people in the US, including immigrants. For gender and/or historical comparisons of aspirations and concerns. 470 pp. Also see: (1972, 1997). *Working: People talk about what they do all day and how they feel about what they do*. New York: Ballantine Books. 750 pp.

Wiener, H. S., & Bazerman, C. (Eds.), (1996). Side by side: A multicultural reader (2nd ed.), Boston, MA: Houghton Mifflin. With key words; discussion, reading and writing tasks.

[3]Gite, L. (1991). Like mother, like daughter. The unique challenges mother-daughter businesses face that father-son or father-daughter companies do not. 1800 wds.

[2]Raybon, P. (1997). Letting in light. A mother passes on to her daughter the family's window washing tradition, a political statement of black women's historic work. 1100 wds.

Fairy tales, legends, myths and traditional stories

[1] Gone is gone. In A. Lurie & M. Tomes (Illus.), (1980), *Clever Gretchen and other forgotten folktales*. New York: Thomas Y. Crowell. Spouses exchange roles, but the husband makes a mess of his chores. 860 wds.

Novels and historical works

[3] Apple, M. W. (1986). Teaching and women's work. In *Teachers and texts*. London: Routledge & Kegan Paul. An historic examination of teaching related to sexual and class divisions in the US and England; with 1923 teacher contract, tables on number of teachers by gender. 7000 wds.

[1] Brown, P. (1989). *Florence Nightingale: The determined English woman who founded modern nursing and reformed military medicine*. Milwaukee, WI: Gareth Stevens. A young British 19th century upper-class woman's struggle to find intellectual stimulation. Although her parents objected to her pursuing math, she studied, worked and found modern nursing. Juvenile book. 68 pp.

[1] Cole, S., & Farrow, T. C.(Illus.). (1991). *The dragon in the cliff: A novel based on the life of Mary Anning*. New York: Lothrop, Lee & Shepard. Born in 1799, Anning is prevented from being recognized for her scientific work, including finding the first complete fossil skeleton of a marine dinosaur-like creature. Juvenile book. 211 pp.

[2] Eisenberg, S. (1999). *We'll call you if we need you: Experiences of women working construction*. Ithaca, NY: ILR Press/Cornell UP. Women breaking into the trades: 30 interviews on, e.g., decisions to enter the trades, first days on the job, strategies to get training. 240 pp.

[1]Grant, L. (1994). *A woman's place*. New York: Charles Scribner's Sons. A contemporary story about sexual harassment in the computerized workplace. Juvenile book. 203 pp.

[2] Halsell, G. (1996). *In their shoes*. Fort Worth, TX: Texas Christian University. Autobiography of 20th century American journalist who wrote "her way around the world" and impersonated US minority women to understand their plight. 252 pp.

[2] Miller, A. (1949). *Death of a salesman*. New York: Penguin. A play about an aging, failing salesman who has unrealistic dreams for his sons and himself. For exploring expectations. Women's small roles are subservient. 139 pp. Video. (1986 US). 118 min.

[2] Schroedel, J.R. (1985). Nora Quealey. In *Alone in a crowd: Women in the trades tell their stories*. Philadelphia, PA: Temple UP. Oral history of a woman unsure about her roles as wife, mother, blue-collar worker. 2600 wds. The book has more interviews of blue-collar women.

Poetry

Annas, P.J., & Rosen, R. C.(Eds.). (1994). *Literature and society: An Introduction to fiction, poetry, drama, nonfiction* (2nd ed.). Englewood Cliffs, NJ: Prentice Hall.

> [2] Grahn, J. (1978). Ella, in a square apron, along Highway 80. The hard life of a waitress at a truck stop. 23 lines.

> [2] Griffin, S. (1976). This is the story of the day in the life of a woman trying. The job of writing always seems interrupted by daily chores and a child home sick. 76 lines.

[2] Eisenberg, S. (1998). *Pioneering: Poems from the construction site*. Ithica, NY: ILR Press/Cornell UP. Poems about construction work, many about women at the worksite. 61 pp.

[1]Glenn, M. (1986). *Class dismissed II: More high school poems*. New York: Clarion Books/Ticknor & Fields. Poems about the emotional lives of contemporary US students.

> Mandy Bailer. A female lifeguard complains of the sex stereotyping by co-workers and those she helps. For exploring gender roles and expectations. 18 lines.

> Amanda Butler. A child's unhappiness at the short cryptic notes her mother leaves family members because she goes to work. 22 lines.

Proverbs

"Behind every successful man, there is a woman."

"A man may work from sun to sun, but a woman's work is never done."

"Every man for himself."

"May the best man win."

"A stitch in time saves nine."

"Women hold up half the sky." (Chinese)

"Take care of number 1."

"Nails that stick out must be hammered in." (Japanese)

"To the winner belong the spoils."

Short stories

[2] Mori, T. (1951). Japanese Hamlet. In J. A. McConochie. (1995). *20th century American short stories* (vol. 2). Boston, MA: Heinle & Heinle. A Japanese American refuses to abandon his dream of becoming a Shakespearean actor and get a regular job; with reading, writing, discussion questions. For exploring gendered and cross-cultural work expectations. 1140 wds.

[2] Saroyan, W. (1986, 1987). The parsley garden. In J. Dennis, *Experiences: Reading literature*. Cambridge, MA: Newbury House. An eleven-year-old boy, with no summer job, steals a hammer, is caught and then works to pay for it. When offered a job, he refuses; instead, he builds a bench for the garden; with glossary, notes, grammar (modals) and retelling tasks, strategy suggestions. 2540 wds.

Media

Magazines and newspapers

Articles and advice columns on work can be found in magazines such as: *Ms, Career Woman, Cosmopolitan,* and *Working Woman.*

Comics and cartoons such as those by Jules Feiffer and Matt Groening are also useful. They can be found in collected works such as:

Heller, S. (Ed.). (1982). *Jules Feiffer's America.* New York: Alfred A. Knopf. Wolf, W. (Ed.). (1986). Groening's *Work is hell.* New York: Pantheon Books.

Groening, M. (1990). *The big book of hell.* New York: Pantheon Books. On childhood, love, school, and work.

Movies on video

Broadcast news. (1987 US). 131 min. Network Washington affiliate operations centers on the ambitions and love triangle of a hollow male anchor, a female producer who falls for him, and a male reporter whom the producer sees as a friend. Also about misplaced love, obsessive behavior and adrenaline addiction. Also *Network.* (1976 US). 121 min.

Norma Rae. (1979 US). 113 min. Mill workers try to unionize. Useful part: To keep firebrand Norma Rae quiet at the mill, she's promoted to spot checker. Due to negative reactions, she quits and returns to her old job.

Working girl. (1988 US). 115 min. An ambitious, bright secretary, not taken seriously by her male bosses, then has a female boss stealing her ideas to further her career. The secretary succeeds.

Television shows

Current shows and reruns present women and men at the workplace, such as: *The Practice, Ally McBeal, NewsRadio, E.R., Frasier, Law & Order, N.Y.P.D. Blue, Suddenly Susan, 3rd Rock from the Sun, Veronica's Closet, Cheers, Designing Women, Murphy Brown.*

REFERENCES

AAUW (1999). *Gender gaps: Where schools still fail our children.* New York: Marlowe and Company.

Arliss, L. P., & Borisoff, D. J. (Eds.) (1993). *Women and men communicating: Challenges and changes.* Fort Worth: Harcourt Brace Jovanovich.

Case, S. S. (1992). Organizational inequity in a steel plant: A language model. In K. Hall, M. Bucholtz, M & B. Moonwoman (Eds.) *Locating power: Proceedings of the second Berkeley women and language conference* (vol. 1, pp. 36-48). Berkeley, CA: Berkeley Women and Language Group, UC Berkeley.

Gabriel, S. L., & Smithson, I. (1990). *Gender in the classroom: Power and pedagogy.* Urbana. IL: University of Illinois Press.

McElhinny, B. S. (1998). 'I don't smile much anymore': Affect, gender and the discourse of Pittsburgh police officers. In J. Coates (Ed.), *Language and gender: A reader* (pp. 309-327). Oxford, England: Blackwell.

Orenstein, P. (1994). *School girls: Young women, self-esteem, and the confidence gap.* New York: Doubleday.

Sadker, M., & Sadker, D. (1982). *Sex equity handbook for schools.* New York: Longman.

Sadker, M., & Sadker, D. (1994). *Failing at fairness: How our schools cheat girls.* New York: Touchstone Press.

Tannen, D. (1994). *Talking from 9 to 5: How women's and men's conversational styles affect who gets heard, who gets credit, and what gets done at work.* New York: William Morrow and Company.

Yepez, M. (1994). An observation of gender-specific teacher behavior in the ESL classroom. *Sex Roles, 30* (1-2), 121-133.

Sample Unit: **Gender Differences in Education**

Goal 2: Exploring gender differences in education, both real and stereotypical, in the US.

Activity 1: Freewriting:
Opportunities in School for Females and Males

Materials: Paper and pen or pencil for each student

Grouping: Whole class; then 3 or 4 students per group

Preparation: Supply the task instructions in writing: *What opportunities in US schools seem unavailable to your gender in schools in your culture? Conversely, what opportunities for your gender exist in your culture's schools but not in the US?*

Procedure: 1. After freewriting, have students form groups.

2. Ask students to share their freewriting. Appoint one student per group to record the group's ideas and questions about US schools or those in their cultures, or have all students use a K-W-L chart: columns for what students know, what they want to learn, and what they learned (this column is done at the unit end).

Activity 2: Video Viewing:
Gendered Behavior in US Schools

Materials: Scenes of a US classroom (*see Annotated Resources*)

Grouping: Two groups; then whole class for video viewing; then groups again

Preparation: Supply the task instructions: *You will be viewing scenes of a US classroom in order to observe gender differences and similarities in the classroom. Half the class will observe the teacher and half observe the students. Before viewing, you will meet with your group to divide up the items to observe from the list I distribute.*

Procedure: 1. Split the students into two groups.

2. Provide each group with the list of teacher behaviors and student behaviors to observe from the Activities in Gender Differences in Education, Goal 2C, to divide up the items. (Several students can collect the same data.)

Procedure:	3. Elicit and/or suggest how students can collect their data (e.g. checking off occurrences, transcribing speech, drawing a chart of the seating).

3. Elicit and/or suggest how students can collect their data (e.g. checking off occurrences, transcribing speech, drawing a chart of the seating).

4. Play the video once. Check that students are able to collect their data. Help students revise their method of data collection if necessary.

5. Replay the video as many times as needed.

6. After viewing, have groups re-form to cull data, draw conclusions, and make recommendations. Supply the new task instructions:

   a. Have each member report to the group on the data collected. All take notes.

   b. Based on these reports, draw conclusions and make recommendations in terms of gender differences and similarities. Appoint a recorder to take notes.

   c. As a team, write a report of what you learned to present to the class. Decide how you will accomplish this report and who will be responsible for each part.

7. Provide instructor's feedback and error treatment.

Activity 3: **Formal Writing: Stereotypes & Realities of Gender Differences in US Education**

Materials: Paper and pen or pencil or computer station for each student

Grouping: Individual seat work; pairs for developing ideas and revising

Preparation: Supply the task instructions in writing: *Students from your culture are considering studying in the US. Persuade them to study or not to study here. Compare the similarities and differences between female and male students in the US. Include stereotyped behaviors compared to your actual experiences in US classes.*

Procedure: 1. Have students create a list or Venn[1] diagram before writing, to help them develop points of comparison.

2. Have student pairs check each other's list or diagram.

3. When students have completed a first draft, have them form pairs again to provide peer feedback on their comparisons.

4. Have students revise their papers before instructor feedback and error treatment.

---

[1] A Venn diagram consists of two overlapping circles for comparing and contrasting two items; students fill in the overlapping segment with similarities and the outer segments with differences.

Sample Unit:	Gender in the Workplace

Goal 3: Examining changing patterns in the workplace related to gender in students' own cultures and US cultures.

Activity 1: Discussion:
Prestigious Professions in Different Cultures

Materials: None

Grouping: Whole class

Preparation: Supply the task instructions: *What are prestigious professions in your culture? Are both women and men in positions of authority in these professions in your culture?*

Procedure: Have students discuss the topic. The instructor can elicit these points: (1) Have these professions always been open to both genders? (2) If not, when did the change take place? What caused the change? (3) Are both genders treated equally by their colleagues, subordinates, and superiors, and by people receiving their services?

Activity 2: Proverbs:
Proverbs as Expressions of Rules of Behavior

Materials: List of proverbs (see below)

Grouping: 3 or 4 students per group

Preparation: Supply the task instructions in writing: *Discuss the meanings of each of the following proverbs in relation to work-related roles of women and men:*

1. Behind every successful man, there is a woman. (US)

2. When the going gets tough, the tough get going. (US)

3. Women hold up half the sky. (Chinese)

4. Nails that stick out must be hammered in. (Japanese)

Afterward, take turns sharing one proverb related to work from each of your cultures. Then have your group members explain each proverb's meaning.

Procedure:
1. Have students discuss the above proverbs and then each share one proverb from their particular culture.

2. Supply the next task instructions: *Select the proverb whose message is most interesting, disturbing, or stereotypical and explain in writing your reaction.*

Activity 3:	Literature: Women and Men in Non-traditional Work
Materials:	Genasci, L. (1996). "Barriers Fall for Women at Work". In B. Wegmann, M. P. Knezevic, & M. Bernstein. *Mosaic Two: A Reading Skills Book*, (3d ed.). New York: McGraw Hill.
Grouping:	Individual work or homework; then groups of 3 or 4 students.
Preparation:	Supply the task instructions: *As you read Genasci's article, make a list of the reasons the author gives for the increase in the number of women in the trades in the US. Prepare to discuss the role of women in the trades in your own cultures.*
Procedure:	1. After reading, have students form groups. Supply the next task instructions: *Review Genasci's reasons for the slow increase in the number of women in US trades. Then discuss the role of women in the trades in your cultures, including if there are changes and why these changes are or are not happening.* 2. Afterward, have students write a brief summary of what they learned from other classmates about the role of women in the trades in various cultures.
Activity 4:	Formal Writing: *Women and Men at Work*
Materials:	Paper and pen or pencil or computer station for each student.
Grouping:	Pairs; then individual work or homework
Preparation:	Supply the task instructions: *Argue for or against women doing more traditional male jobs and males more traditional female jobs. Find a classmate who has the same opinion as you; together brainstorm ideas to support your opinion.*
Procedure:	1. After sharing the assignment, have students form pairs based on the position they are taking in order to brainstorm ideas. 2. With a completed first draft, have pairs provide feedback on supporting details. 3. Have students revise their papers before providing instructor feedback.

ABOUT THE AUTHORS

Joan Lesikin is an accomplished ESL teacher and teacher trainer. Her research interests are in the areas of educational text materials, second language teaching methodologies, second language reading and writing, and the sociology of education. Recent publications include, "Determining Social Prominence: A Methodology for Uncovering Gender Bias in ESL Textbooks" (College ESL, 1998) and "Collaborative Student Roles through Computer Activities: A Low-Budget Approach" (Idiom, 1999). Other articles include "Potential Student Decision Making in Academic ESL Grammar Textbooks" (Linguistics & Education, in press) and "Complex Text in ESL Textbooks: Barriers or Gateways?" (Reading in a Foreign Language, in press).

Alice H. Deakins is a Professor of English at William Paterson University, Wayne NJ. She teaches courses in linguistics, literature, and women's studies, and co-directed the Women's Studies Program there for several years. For the past 17 years, she has taught a summer graduate course in gender and language at Teachers College, Columbia University. Her areas of research are gender and language and pedagogical grammar. She has published articles on gender and is co-author of The Tapestry Grammmar (Heinle & Heinle 1994). She is currently co-editing an anthology Mother-Daughter Communication: Voices from the Professions.